1

Published by PasstheCFAexam.com

Topic 1: Professional Standards and Ethics

Standard I: Professionalism

Standard II: Integrity of Capital Markets

Standard III: Duties to Clients

Standard IV: Duties to Employers

Standard V: Investment Analysis, Recommendations, and Actions

Standard VI: Conflicts of Interest

Topics 2 to 8

Part One, Introduction to Alternative Investments, Chapters 1 – 7

Chapter 1: What is an Alternative Investment?

Chapter 2: The Environment of Alternative Investments

Chapter 3: Statistical Foundations

Chapter 4: Risk, Return, and Benchmarking

Chapter 5: Correlation, Alternative Returns, and Performance Measurement

Chapter 6: Alpha and Beta

Chapter 7: Hypothesis Testing in Alternative Investments

Part Two – Real Assets, Chapters 8 – 10

Chapter 8: Land, Infrastructure, and Intangible Real Assets

Chapter 9: Real Estate Fixed-Income Investments

Chapter 10: Real Estate Equity Investments

Part Three – Hedge Funds, Chapters 11 – 17

Chapter 11: Introduction to Hedge Funds

Chapter 12: Hedge Fund Returns and Asset Allocation

Chapter 13: Macro and Managed Futures Funds

Chapter 14: Event-Driven Hedge Funds

Topic 1: Professional Standards and Ethics

Keywords

Additional compensation: Refers to compensation granted to an employee by anyone other than their employer.

Best execution: The responsibility of brokers to provide the most advantageous order execution for their customers. Best execution requires brokers to get the best price for a trade in the shortest time frame.

Blackout/restricted periods: Times when you are prohibited from trading your company's securities (in contrast to window periods are times when you are allowed to trade. Some companies also prohibit option exercises during blackouts. A company may impose a blackout when it believes that insiders possess material nonpublic information. Blackouts can occur at regular intervals, such as before earnings announcements, or can arise because of sudden events, such as merger negotiations. They usually occur for a shorter period for rank-and-file employees than for executives.

Block allocation: large allocation of stock or bonds

Block trades: large trade of stocks or bonds

Brokerage: trading on behalf of clients

Buy-side: The people that actually manage money (pensions, hedge funds) or buy investment services

Commissions: What the client pays a broker to execute a trade on their behalf

Composites: Aggregation of multiple portfolios managed to similar investment mandate

Custody: Specialized financial institution responsible for safeguarding a firm's or individual's financial assets.

Directed brokerage: Client directs its adviser to use commissions to obtain products or services that are used by the client.

Disclosure: The act of releasing all relevant information pertaining to a company that may influence an investment decision.

Due diligence: An investigation or audit of a potential investment done prior to investing.

Execution of orders: When an investor places a trade, whether online or over the phone, the order goes to a broker. The broker then looks at the size and availability of the order to decide which path is the best way for it to be executed. With a market order, speed and price execution is very important.

Fair dealing: Members must deal fairly and objectively with all clients and prospects when providing investment analysis, making investment recommendations, taking investment action, or in other professional activities.

Firewalls: The ethical barrier between different divisions of a financial (or other) institution to avoid conflict of interest.

"Flash" report: Periodic snapshot of key financial and operational data. It's a one-page report that helps management assess the key performance indicators of the company. Divided into liquidity, productivity and profitability sections. The Liquidity Section tells management about the cash situation of the firm. Is the company generating cash? Does it have enough money to pay the bills? The Productivity Section gives an indication of the key performance metrics of the business. These metrics are tied to operations and are a way to combine the operations of a company to its financial performance. The Profitability Section gives a rough indication of how much money the company has made during the period of measure.

Fraud: Intentional deception made for personal gain or to damage another individual. Fraud may also be made by an omission or purposeful failure to state material facts, which nondisclosure makes other statements misleading.

Front-running: The unethical practice of a broker trading an equity based on information from the analyst department before his or her clients have been given the information. It is also when brokers trade on their own behalf before trading on behalf of clients.

Global Investment Performance Standards (GIPS): Standardized, industry-wide approach for investment firms to follow in calculating and presenting historical investment results to prospects

"Hot issue" securities: A new security issue (e.g. IPO) for which investor demand exceeds securities available.

Incentive fees: A performance-based fee paid to a fund manager by investors.

Independent contractors: A natural person, business, or corporation that provides goods or services to another entity under terms specified in a contract or within a verbal agreement typically on a freelance basis. Independent contractors are self-employed and typically do not receive employment benefits (e.g. medical, dental) like employees.

Insider trading: The buying or selling of a security by someone who has access to material, nonpublic information about the security.

Market manipulation: Practices intended to mislead market participants through distorted prices or artificially inflated trading volume

Material changes: A change in the affairs of a company that is expected to affect the market value of its securities (e.g. change in the nature of the business, a change in senior principal officers, etc.). A material change must be reported to the applicable self-regulatory organization.

Material nonpublic information: Members and Candidates in possession of nonpublic information that could affect an investment's value must not act or induce someone else to act on the information. Information is "material" if its disclosure would impact the price of a security or if reasonable investors would want the information before making an investment decision.

Misappropriation: The act of stealing confidential information from an employer and then trading securities based on the misappropriated insider knowledge.

Mosaic theory: When an analyst reaches an investment conclusion about a corporate action or event through an analysis of public information together with items of non-material non-public information. No violation of insider trading as a result.

Oversubscribed issue: A situation in which the demand for an initial public offering (IPO) of securities exceeds the total number of shares issued.

Performance fees: See 'Incentive Fee' definition above

Plagiarism: Taking another's work or ideas and presenting them as your own.

Pump and dump: artificially inflating the price of an owned stock through false and misleading positive statements, in order to sell the cheaply purchased stock at a higher price.

Referral fees: Compensation received from a third party in exchange for referring business to that party.

Restricted list: A list that may be compiled that prohibits trading in companies that have engaged that firm in a business relationship (e.g. underwriter for an IPO).

Round-lot: A group of 100 shares of a stock, or any group of shares that can be evenly divided by 100, such as 300 or 50,000.

Secondary offerings: The issuance of new stock for public sale from a company that has already made its initial public offering (IPO).

Secondary research: Research obtained from another party within the firm.

Self-dealing: Conduct of a trustee, an attorney, a corporate officer, or other fiduciary that consists of taking advantage of his position in a transaction and acting for his own interests rather than for the interests of the beneficiaries of the trust, corporate shareholders, or his clients. Form of conflict of interest.

Sell-side: companies that sell investment services (e.g. investment banks)

Soft commissions / Soft dollars: Any type of commission that is not paid in actual dollars. Soft commissions allow investment companies and institutional funds to cover some of their expenses through trading commissions. For example, receiving research from a counterparty in exchange for using their brokerage services. Thus the expense would be classified as trading commissions and at the same time would lower their reported expenses on research in this instance.

Thinly traded security: An inactive or infrequently traded bond or stock.

Watch list: A list of securities being monitored closely by a brokerage or exchange in order to spot irregularities or a list of securities being monitored for potential trading or investing opportunities.

Whisper number: "Unofficial and unpublished earnings per share (EPS) forecasts that circulate among professionals on Wall Street. Because the whisper number is the analysts' true expectation, it tends to be more accurate than the officially published consensus estimates.

Whistle-blowing: The disclosure by a person, usually an employee in a government agency or private enterprise, to the public or to those in authority, of mismanagement, corruption, illegality, or some other wrongdoing.

Code of Ethics

1   Act with integrity, competence, diligence, respect, and in an ethical manner with the public, clients, prospective clients, employers, employees, colleagues in the investment profession, and other participants in the global capital markets.

2   Place the integrity of the investment profession and the **interests of clients** above their own personal interests.

3   Use reasonable care and exercise **independent** professional judgment when conducting investment analysis, making investment recommendations, taking investment actions, and engaging in other professional activities.

4   Practice and encourage others to practice in a professional and ethical manner that will **reflect credit** on themselves and the profession.

5   Promote the integrity of, and uphold the rules governing, capital markets.

6   Maintain and improve their professional competence and strive to maintain and improve the competence of other investment professionals.

Standards of Professional Conduct

1   **Professionalism** - know the law, objectivity, misrepresentation, misconduct

2   **Integrity of Capital Markets**– nonpublic information, market manipulation

3   **Duties to Clients** - put them first, suitability, performance presentation

4   **Duties to Employers** –additional compensation, whistle-blowing

5   **Investment Analysis, Recommendations, and Action** – fact vs. opinion, diligence, record retention

6   **Conflicts of Interest** – priority of transactions (clients and employers before CFA members)

7   **Responsibilities as a CFA Institute Member or CFA Candidate**

Standard I: Professionalism

A. Knowledge of the Law

Members must understand and comply with laws, rules, regulations, and Code and Standards of any authority governing their activities. In the event of a conflict, follow the more strict law, rule, or regulation. Do not knowingly participate or assist in violations, and disassociate from any known violation.

Members must know the laws and regulations relating to their professional activities in all countries in which they conduct business. Members must comply with applicable laws and regulations relating to their professional activity. Do not violate Code or Standards even if the activity is otherwise legal. Always adhere to the most strict rules and requirements (law or CFA Institute Standards) that apply.

Members should disassociate or separate themselves from any ongoing client or employee activity that is illegal or unethical, even if it involves leaving an employer (an extreme case). While a member may confront the involved individual first, he must approach his supervisor or compliance department. Inaction with continued association may be construed as knowing participation.

B. Independence and Objectivity.

Members and Candidates must use reasonable care and judgment to exercise independence and objectivity in professional activities. Members and Candidates are not to offer, solicit, or accept any gift, benefit, compensation, or consideration that would compromise either their own or someone else's independence and objectivity.

Do not let the investment process be influenced by any external sources. Modest gifts are permitted. **Allocation of shares in oversubscribed IPOs to personal accounts for members and candidates is**

NOT permitted. Distinguish between gifts from clients and gifts from entities seeking influence to the detriment of the client. Gifts must be *disclosed* to the member's employer in any case.

Example: Private gifts – even if sent to your office –are fine if they are not likely to affect your professional activities.

- **Investment banking relationships regarding research; public companies, travel funding**

C. Misrepresentation

Members and Candidates must not knowingly misrepresent facts regarding investment analysis, recommendations, actions, or other professional activities.

Trust is a foundation in the investment profession. Do not make any misrepresentations or give false impressions. This includes oral and electronic communications. Misrepresentations include guaranteeing investment performance and plagiarism. Plagiarism encompasses using someone else's work (e.g., reports, forecasts, charts, graphs, and spreadsheet models) without giving them credit.

- Don't misrepresent credentials, qualifications; plagiarism; work completed for employer and using work done by others (hyping up what you did vs. what the team did)

Example: You also need to correct someone if they assume that you completed something or came up with an idea that wasn't your own.

D. Misconduct

Members and Candidates must not engage in any professional(personal doesn't matter) conduct involving dishonesty, fraud, or deceit or commit any act that reflects adversely on their integrity, good reputation, trustworthiness, or professional competence.

CFA Institute discourages unethical behavior in all aspects of members' and candidates' lives. Do not abuse CFA Institute's Professional Conduct Program by seeking enforcement of this Standard to settle personal, political, or other disputes that are not related to professional ethics.

Standard II: Integrity of Capital Markets

A. Material Nonpublic Information

Members and Candidates in possession of nonpublic information that could affect an investment's value must not act or induce someone else to act on the information.

Information is "material" if its disclosure would impact the price of a security or if reasonable investors would want the information before making an investment decision. Ambiguous information, as far as its likely effect on price, may not be considered material. Information is "non-public" until it has been made available to the marketplace. An analyst conference call is not public disclosure. Selectively disclosing information by corporations creates the potential for insider-trading violations.

Mosaic theory: There is no violation when a perceptive analyst reaches an investment conclusion about a corporate action or event through an analysis of public information together with items of non-material non-public information.

Recommended procedure: Add securities to the firm's *restricted list* when the firm has or may have material nonpublic information. Keep departments physically separate; have firewalls; analysts should issue press releases before meetings and conference calls; analysts/management should script the calls

Example: Blogs and company websites are in the public domain and do not constitute inside information. You can also use these to supplement your research process.

B.   Market Manipulation

Members and Candidates must not engage in any practices intended to mislead market participants through distorted prices or artificially inflated trading volume. Spreading false rumors is also prohibited.

This Standard applies to transactions that deceive the market by distorting the price-setting mechanism of financial instruments or by securing a controlling position to manipulate the price of a related derivative and/or the asset itself.

Standard III: Duties to Clients

A.   Loyalty, Prudence, and Care

Members must always act for the benefit of clients and place clients' interests before their employer's or their own interests. Members must be loyal to clients, use reasonable care, and exercise prudent judgment.

Identify who the client actually is (person, trust, etc.) → duty of loyalty

Client interests always come first.

- Determine and comply with any applicable fiduciary duty to clients.
- Exercise the prudence, care, skill, and diligence under the circumstances that a person acting in a like capacity and familiarity with such matters would use.
- Manage pools of client assets in accordance with the terms of the governing documents, such as trust documents or investment management agreements.
- Make investment decisions in the context of the total portfolio.
- Vote proxies in an informed and responsible manner. Due to cost benefit considerations, it may not be necessary to vote all proxies.
- Client brokerage, or "soft dollars" or "soft commissions" must be used to benefit the client.

Example: Doesn't matter if a brokerage firm also provides research information that is not useful to the account generating the commission if the client is not paying extra money for that information.

B.   Fair Dealing

Members must deal fairly and objectively with all clients and prospects when providing investment analysis, making investment recommendations, taking investment action, or in other professional activities.

Do not discriminate against any clients when disseminating recommendations or taking investment action. Fairly does not mean equally. In the normal course of business, there will be differences in the time e-mails, faxes, etc. are received by different clients. Different service levels are okay, but they must not negatively affect or disadvantage any clients. Disclose the different service levels to all clients and prospects, and make premium levels of service available to all who wish to pay for them.

Give all clients a fair opportunity to act upon every recommendation. Clients who are unaware of a change in a recommendation should be advised before the order is accepted. Calling favored clients subsequent to distribution of the change in recommendation is **not** a violation as long as they are not given pre-notification of the change.

Investment recommendations: ensure that information is disseminated in a way that all clients have a fair opportunity to act on every recommendation.

Investment action (for PMs): allocate blocks of stock fairly; must ***prorate*** oversubscribed issues (e.g. IPOs); can't over-allocate to a particular client.

Recommended **policy:** develop firm procedures; disclose trade allocation procedures. Firm policy about partially executed block trades to be allocated pro-rata subject to minimum lot size is a *recommendation* not a requirement and only applies to members and candidates.

C. Suitability – **diversify! If managing to an index, stick to mandate**
   a. When in an advisory relationship with client or prospect, Members and Candidates must:
      a. Make reasonable inquiry into clients' investment experience, risk and return objectives, and constraints prior to making any recommendations or taking investment action. Reassess information and update regularly.
      b. Be sure investments are suitable to a client's financial situation and consistent with client objectives before making recommendation or taking investment action.
      c. Make sure investments are suitable in the context of a client's total portfolio.
   b. When managing a portfolio, investment recommendations and actions must be consistent with the stated portfolio objectives and constraints.

Update investment policy at least **annually** and before material changes to any specific recommendations or decisions on behalf of the client. Should *encourage* firm to adhere to GIPS although there are other ways to comply besides GIPS.

D. Performance Presentation

Analysts can promote the success or accuracy or recommendations but presentations (or distributing materials) of investment performance information must be fair, **accurate**, and complete.

Members must avoid misstating performance or misleading clients/prospects about investment performance of themselves or their firms, should not misrepresent past performance or reasonably expected performance, and should not state or imply the ability to achieve a rate of return similar to that achieved in the past.

Example: When presenting performance you have to disclose that you were part of a team that achieved the results shown. If you only include the potion that you directly manage, not a violation.

E. Preservation of Confidentiality

All information about current and former clients and prospects must be kept confidential unless it pertains to illegal activities, disclosure is required by law, the client or prospect gives permission for the information to be disclosed, or when cooperating with a CFA Institute Professional Conduct Program (PCP) investigation.

If illegal activities by a client are involved, members may have an obligation to report the activities to authorities. The confidentiality Standard extends to former clients as well.

Status of client: keep client records confidential even if no longer a client

Standard IV: Duties to Employers

A. Loyalty

In matters related to their employment, Members and Candidates must act for the benefit of their employer and not deprive their employer of the advantage of their skills and abilities, divulge confidential information, or otherwise cause harm to their employer.

Members must not engage in any activities which would injure the firm, deprive it of profit, or deprive it of the advantage of employees' skills and abilities. Always place client interests above interests of employer. There is no requirement that the employee put employer interests ahead of family and other personal obligations.

Independent practice for compensation is allowed if a notification is provided to the employer fully describing all aspects of the services AND you receive employer consent.

Leaving an employer: Members must continue to act in their employer's best interests until resignation is effective.

Whistleblowing: There may be isolated cases where a duty to one's employer may be violated in order to protect clients or the integrity of the market, and <u>not for personal gain</u>.

Example: When you leave an employer, you can't take records or files (including models) without the written permission of the employer. Watch behavior in contrast to company compliance procedures.

B. Additional Compensation Arrangements

No gifts, benefits, compensation, or consideration are to be accepted which may create a conflict of interest with the employer's interest unless written consent is received from all parties. If this is not the case, written consent is NOT needed.

Compensation includes direct and indirect compensation from a client and other benefits received from third parties. Written consent from a member's employer includes e-mail communication.

C. Responsibilities of Supervisors

All Members and Candidates must make reasonable efforts to detect and prevent violations of laws, rules, regulations, and the Code and Standards by any person under their supervision or authority.

Members must take steps to prevent employees from violating laws, rules, regulations, or the Code and Standards and make reasonable efforts to detect violations.

Understand that an adequate compliance system must meet industry standards, regulatory requirements, and the requirements of the Code and Standards. Members with supervisory responsibilities have an obligation to bring an inadequate compliance system to the attention of firm's management and recommend corrective action. While investigating a possible breach of compliance procedures, it is appropriate to limit the suspected employee's activities.

Requires that during the investigation of wrongdoing, steps must be taken to ensure that the violation will not be repeated. The appropriate steps are to limit the employee's activities and/or increase the monitoring of the employee during the investigation of wrongdoing. The Standard does **not** require specific sanctions or detail how or when they should be applied (e.g. severity of punishment for first-time offenders vs. otherwise).

Responsibilities of Supervisors requires anyone **delegating** supervisory responsibility to instruct those employees in how to prevent and detect violations of the firm's compliance policies and procedures.

-   **If firm lacks adequate compliance system, should decline to accept supervisory role in writing**

Standard V: Investment Analysis, Recommendations, and Actions

A. Diligence and Reasonable Basis

When analyzing investments, making recommendations, and taking investment actions use diligence, independence, and thoroughness.

Investment analysis, recommendations, and actions should have a reasonable and adequate basis, supported by research and investigation.

The application of this Standard depends on the investment philosophy adhered to, Members' and Candidates' roles in the investment decision-making process, and the resources and support provided by employers. These factors dictate the degree of diligence, thoroughness of research, and the proper level of investigation required.

Using secondary (someone else in the firm) or third-party (outside of the firm) research: See that the research is sound.

Group research and decision making: Even if a Member does not agree with the independent and objective view of the group, he does not necessarily have to decline to be identified with the report, as long as there is a reasonable and adequate basis.

Example: Hearing the opinion of another financial analyst is not a *reasonable and adequate basis* for changing your recommendation. If overhearing an opinion sparks you to do additional research that justified a change of opinion → no violation (not a distinguishing fact from opinion issue).

B. Communication with Clients and Prospective Clients

Disclose to clients AND prospects basic format and general principles of investment processes used to analyze and select securities and construct portfolios. Promptly disclose any process changes. Outline and identify limitations of analysis.

Use reasonable judgment in identifying relevant factors important to investment analyses, recommendations, or actions, and include factors when communicating with clients and prospects.

Investment analyses and recommendations should clearly differentiate facts from opinions.

Estimates, outlooks and forecasts are OPINIONS subject to future circumstances.

Proper communication with clients is critical to provide quality financial services. Members must distinguish between opinions and facts and always include the basic characteristics of the security being analyzed in a research report.

Members must illustrate to clients and prospects the investment decision-making process utilized. The suitability of each investment is important in the context of the entire portfolio.

All means of communication are included here, not just research reports.

C. Record Retention

Maintain all records supporting analysis, recommendations, actions, and all other investment-related communications with clients and prospects.

Members must maintain research records that support the reasons for the analyst's conclusions and any investment actions taken. Such records are the property of the firm. If no other regulatory standards are in place, CFA Institute **recommends at least a 7-year holding period.**

Standard VI: Conflicts of Interest

- Disclose
- Types of conflicts: cross-departments; stock ownership, director
- Priority of transactions – put client first
- Referral fees – must disclose BEFORE entering into formal agreement with client

Standard VII: Responsibilities as a CFA Institute Member or CFA Candidate

A. Conduct as Members and Candidates in the CFA Program

Can't disclose even broad topical areas of the exam.

Members and Candidates must not engage in any conduct that compromises the reputation or integrity of CFA Institute or the CFA designation or the integrity, validity, or security of the CFA exams.

This Standard applies to conduct which includes:

- Cheating on the CFA exam or any exam.
- Not following rules and policies of the CFA program.
- Giving confidential information on the CFA exam to Candidates or the public.
- Improperly using the designation to further personal and professional goals.
- Misrepresenting information on the Professional Conduct Statement (PCS) or the CFA Institute Professional Development Program.

Members and candidates are **NOT** precluded from expressing their opinions regarding the exam program or CFA Institute.

> B. Reference to CFA Institute, the CFA Designation, and the CFA Program.

Members and Candidates must not misrepresent or exaggerate the meaning or implications of membership in CFA Institute, holding the CFA designation, or candidacy in the program.

Members must **not** make promotional promises or guarantees tied to the CFA designation. Do not over-promise individual competence or investment results in the future (i.e., higher performance, less risk, etc.).

Members must satisfy these requirements to maintain membership: (1) sign PCS annually and (2) pay CFA Institute membership dues annually. If they fail to do this, they are no longer active members.

Do not misrepresent or exaggerate the meaning of the designation.

There is no partial designation. It **is** acceptable to state that a Candidate successfully completed the program in three years, if in fact they did, but claiming superior ability because of this is not permitted.

The Chartered Financial Analyst and CFA marks must always be used either after a charterholder's name or as adjectives, but not as nouns, in written and oral communications.

CFA Institute Soft Dollar Standards

> A. Define soft-dollar arrangements, and state the general principles of the Soft Dollar Standards.

Soft dollars can only be used to benefit THAT client.

CFA Institute's Soft Dollar Standards are **not mandatory**. Soft Dollar requirements (e.g. execution, disclosure, etc.) are only required behavior only if the firm wants to _claim compliance_ with the Soft Dollar Standards.

Soft Dollars, including both agency (payment of an explicit commission) and principal trades (discount or a spread), involve the use of client brokerage by an investment manager to obtain certain products and services to aid the manager in the investment decision-making process.

The investment manager should consider that:

- The manager is a fiduciary and as such must disclose all details relating to benefits received through a client's brokerage.
- Third-party and proprietary research are to be treated similarly when examining soft dollar arrangements because the research received is paid for with client brokerage.
- Any research purchased with client brokerage must directly assist the investment manager in the investment process and not in the overall management of the firm.
- If there is ever any question as to whether the research assists in the investment process, it should be paid for with investment manager assets.

2 fundamental principles of soft dollars

1. Client commissions paid to a broker are the property of the **client**
2. The quality of the transaction (**execution and cost**) comes first – balance both of these factors; object not necessarily to minimize cost. Directing brokerage to preferred brokers is FINE if the preferred broker offers best quality of transaction.

B. Evaluate company soft-dollar practices and policies.

Client-directed brokerage is permissible provided that the manager does not use brokerage from another client to pay for products or services purchased under any client-directed brokerage agreement.

In the case of **client-directed** brokerage there is *no requirement* that the goods and services aid in the investment decision making process. As long as the client is the account beneficiary, the brokerage is the property of the client and can be used as the client wishes.

Recommended procedures: In the case of client-directed brokerage, Standards recommend that the investment manager disclose his duty to continue to seek the best execution since the client-directed brokerage arrangement may impair his ability to do that. Investment managers should also request written instructions that restate the manager's continuing responsibility to seek the best execution.

Disclosure requirements address clarity, discussion of *principal trades* (whether principal or not, etc.), types/sources of research received via proprietary or 3rd party arrangements, annual updates, extent of use, whether an affiliate broker is used and additional information on request.

Record-keeping requirements address the following:

- Legal/regulatory items, timeliness, and broker arrangements.
- Obligations to generate a specific amount of brokerage.
- Mixed use services/products and client-specific disclosures/authorizations/arrangements (including soft dollar or client-directed brokerage).

- Connection among services/products and the investment process.
- Record of compliance with the CFA Institute Soft Dollar Standards and the personnel responsible.

C. Determine whether a product or service qualifies as "permissible research" that can be purchased with client brokerage.

CFA Institute Soft Dollar Standards set forth a 3-level analysis to assist the investment manager in the determination of whether a product or service is "research."

- Level I—Define the Product/Service: Define it in detail, including multiple components. For example, a computer workstation may be classified as a qualifying product, but the electricity to run the equipment would not.
- Level II—Determine (Primary) Usage of the Product or Service: For example, does the Bloomberg service received directly assist in the investment decision-making process, or is it there just to provide an "overall benefit to the firm"?
- Level III—Mixed Use Analysis: This step is only completed if the product or service is classified as "research" based on the Level I and Level II analysis above. This is the investment manager's allocation of the portion of the product or service which directly assists in the investment decision-making process. For example, if the Bloomberg service is used 50% of the time to "determine market and industry trends as part of the investment manager's investment decision-making process," then half of the expense can be paid from client brokerage (firm pays other 50%).

Soft dollars can only be used to pay for research used in investment decision making process. If manager can't determine whether expenditure qualifies for soft dollar, soft dollars can't be used.

CFA Institute Research Objectivity Standards

A. Explain the objectives of the Research Objectivity Standards.

When designing policies and procedures for a firm, strive to achieve these objectives while implementing the CFA Institute Research Objectivity Standards:

- Prepare research; make recommendations; take investment actions; and develop policies, procedures, and disclosures that put client interests before employees' and the firm's interests.
- Facilitate full, fair, meaningful, and specific disclosures to clients and prospects of possible and actual conflicts of interest of the firm and its employees.
- Promote the use of effective policies and procedures that minimize possible conflicts that may adversely affect independence and objectivity of research.
- Support self-regulation by *voluntarily* adhering to specific, measurable standards to promote objective and independent research.
- Provide a work environment conducive to ethical behavior and adherence to the Code and Standards.

Analysts can accept reimbursements for expenses from clients if disclosed to employer

Recommended procedures: update research reports *quarterly*, *restrict employee trades* 30 calendar days before and 5 calendar days after release of research report. Prohibit communication between research and IB. when coverage of a subject company is being discontinued, firms should issue a final research report and recommendation.

    B. Evaluate company policies and practices related to research objectivity, and distinguish between changes required and changes recommended for compliance with the Research Objectivity Standards.

Applies to sell-side research firms (IB, B/D); need senior officer who annually attests to policy adherence

The Research Objectivity Standards contain requirements and recommended compliance procedures concerning:

1. Research Objectivity Policy – formal written policy must be available to clients and prospects and disseminated to all employees
   a. Requires that a senior officer of the firm attest to all clients and prospects that the firm has implemented and adhered to the policy. The Standard does *not* include a requirement for statements by individual employees.
2. Public Appearances – professionals who publicly discuss research must disclose personal and firm conflicts
3. Reasonable and Adequate Basis – research must be reviewed & approved by individual or group
4. Investment Banking
5. Research Analyst Compensation – analyst compensation can't be *directly* linked to IB activities
   a. Requires that compensation must be aligned with both overall research quality and the accuracy of recommendations over time.
   b. E.g. The Antares plan only measures quality at the time the research is issued, rather than over time as is required.
   c. Only *direct* linking of analyst compensation with investment banking/corporate finance activities is prohibited. If analyst compensation *is* dependent on investment banking revenues, this arrangement should be disclosed.
6. Relationships With Subject Companies – can't promise subject companies a favorable report; recommended that firm has policies that require approval from compliance before sharing any information with subject companies.
7. Personal Investments and Trading – no specific *requirement* related to reporting personal holdings. Cannot trade inconsistent with recommendations.
   a. *Required* that firms prohibit employees from purchasing securities of <u>subject companies assigned to them</u> or <u>companies in the industries that they follow</u> *prior* to an IPO. The Research Objectivity Standards do **not** require that firms prohibit covered employees and their immediate families from participating in subject company IPOs in any case.
8. Timeliness of Research Reports and Recommendations – must issue research on subject company on a timely and regular basis.
9. Compliance and Enforcement

10. Disclosure – *not* required to disclose activities in violation to clients & prospects but *recommended*. MUST disclose conflicts.
11. Rating System – must be useful to investors to determine suitability.

Introduction to the Global Investment Performance Standards(GIPS)

What GIPS is

- Standardized, industry-wide approach for investment firms to follow in calculating and presenting historical investment results to prospects.
- Requires use of composites – aggregation of multiple portfolios managed to similar investment mandate (can't cherry pick)

GIPS Compliance

- Compliance is voluntary and only investment management firms that *actually manage assets* can claim compliance
- Plan sponsors and consultants that don't manage assets can claim to endorse standards or require their investment managers to do so
- Compliance is firm-wide and can't be claimed on just a single product
- Verification must be done by third party

Global Investment Performance Standards (GIPS)

Why GIPS is needed

- Standardize calculation & presentation of investment performance
- Firms in countries w/ minimal performance standards can compete for business on an equal footing with firms from countries with tougher standards

GIPS Standards

- Require firms to include all actual, discretionary, fee-paying portfolios in at least one composite defined by investment mandate
- Firms required to present at least five years of GIPS-compliant investment performance. After the minimum, must present up to 10-yr minimum
- If laws conflict with GIPS, must obey law

Role of country sponsors

- Promote GIPS Standards locally
- Provide local market support & input for GIPS Standards
- Present country-specific issues to GIPS committee
- Participate in governance of GIPS Standards via membership in GIPS council and RIPS

Provisions of GIPS Standards

0. Fundamentals of Compliance
    a. Definition of the firm
        i. Creates defined boundaries whereby firm assets can be determined
        ii. Should use broadest definition possible (all regions, offices operating under the brand name regardless of actual name of subsidiary)
    b. Definition of firm discretion
        i. Establishes criteria for which portfolios should be included in composite & based on firm's ability to implement investment strategy
    c. Statements saying that calculation methods are "in compliance" or "consistent" with GIPS are prohibited
1. Input data
    a. Consistency of input data used to calculate performance
    b. Fixed income valuation must include accrues income
    c. For periods on/after Jan 1,2001 – portfolio valuations done monthly
    d. For periods on/after Jan 1,2010 – on the date of al large cash flows
2. Calculation methodology
    a. Uniformity in calculating returns across firms
    b. For periods after Jan 1,2006 – returns reported quarterly
    c. For periods after Jan 1,2010 – returns reported annual
3. Composite construction
    a. Asset-weighted performance of all portfolios in composite
    b. Non-discretionary portfolios NOT included in composites
4. Disclosure
    a. Firm must appropriately use claim of GIPS compliance
    b. Claim of compliance can only be used in a compliant presentation
5. Presentation and reporting
    a. Must indicate percentage of composite assets represented by non-fee paying portfolios or bundled fees, if applicable
    b. Must present gross of fee returns
6. Real Estate
    a. Certain parts of sections 0-5 don't apply
    b. The following not considered RE: publicly-traded RE securities, CMBS, private RE debt
    c. For periods on/after Jan 1,2008 – must be valued quarterly
    d. For RE CEFs, must calculate Since Inception IRR (SI-IRR) using at least quarterly cash flows
7. Private equity
    a. Certain parts of sections 0-5 don't apply
8. Wrap fee / SMA

Topic 2: Introduction to Alternative Investments

Chapter 1: What is an Alternative Investment?

Keywords

Absolute return products: Returns should be analyzed on an absolute basis rather than relative to returns of traditional investments. They have little to no correlation with traditional assets.

Absolute return standard: When returns are evaluated independent of performance in equity or debt markets.

Active management: Efforts of buying and selling securities with the intent of earning superior risk-adjusted return.

Active return: The difference between the return of a portfolio and its benchmark that is due to active management.

Active risk: Risk that causes a portfolio's return to deviate from the return of a benchmark due to active management.

Alternative investment: Any investment that is not simply a long position in traditional investments.

Arbitrage: The attempt to earn *risk-free* profits through the simultaneous purchase and sale of identical positions trading at different prices in different markets.

Benchmark: Performance standard for an index or portfolio that reflects the preferences of an investor with regard to risk and return.

Benchmark return: Return of the benchmark index or benchmark portfolio.

Commodities: Investments distinguished by their emphasis on futures contracts, physical commodities or both.

Compensation structures: Describes the fee structures used to compensate managers.

Distressed debt: Debt of companies that have filed or are likely to file for bankruptcy protection.

Diversifiers: Synonymous with alternative investments. They have the potential to diversify risk in a portfolio.

Efficiency: Tendency of market prices to reflect all available information.

Financial asset: The opposite of a real asset. A direct claim on cash flows such as provided by a share of stock or bond.

Hedge funds: Privately organized investment vehicle that uses its less regulated nature to generate investment opportunities that are substantially distinct from opportunities offered by traditional investment vehicles.

Illiquidity: An investment that trades infrequently and/or with low volume.

Inefficiency: The deviation of actual valuations from anticipated valuations given an efficient market.

Infrastructure investments: Claims on the income of toll roads, regulated utilities, ports, airports, and other real assets traditionally held by the government.

Institutional quality alternative investments: The type of investment that institutions (pensions, endowments) might include in their portfolios. For example, they may hold private equity but would not hold baseball cards or stamps.

Institutional structures: Refers to the extent that an investment is held by institutions.

Investment: An outlay of cash made with the prospect of receiving future benefits.

Leverage Buyouts (LBOs): Transactions in which the equity of a publicly-traded company is purchased using a small amount of equity and a large amount of debt in order to take the firm private.

Lumpy assets: Assets that can be bought and sold only in specific quantities (e.g. large real estate).

Mezzanine debt: Positioned in the capital structure between senior secured debt and equity. Refers to preferred stock, convertible debt and debt with equity kickers.

Normal distribution: Common bell-shaped distribution of returns that is symmetrical with decreasing probabilities of extreme events. In a normal distribution, the mean, median and mode are equal.

Passive investing: Buying and holding securities to match the risk and return of a benchmark, like an index.

Private equity: Equity and debt that are not publicly traded.

Real assets: Focuses on investments in which the underlying assets involve direct ownership of nonfinancial assets.

Real estate: Land and improvements that are permanently affixed, like buildings.

Regulatory structures: Government's role in influencing the nature of an investment via regulation and taxation.

Relative return standard: When returns are evaluated relative to a benchmark.

Return diversifier: If the primary objective of including an investment product in a portfolio is for the reduction in the portfolio's risk due to its lack of correlation with the other assets in the portfolio.

Return enhancer: If the primary objective of including an investment product in a portfolio is the superior average returns that it is believed to offer.

Securities structures: The structuring of cash flows through securitization.

Structured products: Instruments created to exhibit a particular return, risk, taxation, or other attributes.

Timberland: Includes both the land and timber of forests of tree species typically used in the forest products industry.

Trading structures: Role of an investment vehicle's investment managers in developing and implementing trading strategies. (e.g. buy-and-hold vs. fast-paced strategy)

Traditional investments: Long positions in equities, bonds and cash.

Venture capital: Support via equity financing to start-up companies unable to attract capital from traditional sources such as banks or public capital markets.

Learning Objectives

1.1 Demonstrate knowledge of the differences between alternative investments and traditional investments.

For example:

Identify the distinguishing characteristics of institutional quality alternative investments

- The types of investments that institutions (pensions, endowments) would include in their portfolios
- They are less likely to include collectibles or investments in very small and very speculative projects

Recognize traditional and alternative investments

- Traditional: Typically includes long positions in stocks, bonds and cash
- Alternative: Anything outside of traditional investments (private equity, hedge funds)

1.2 Demonstrate knowledge of various alternative investment types.

For example:

Describe real assets (i.e., real estate, land, infrastructure, and intangible assets)and distinguish real assets from financial assets

Real assets focus on investments in which the underlying assets involve direct ownership of nonfinancial assets while financial assets represent a direct claim on cash flows such as provided by a share of stock or bond.

Describe hedge funds/ Describe commodities / Describe private equity / Describe structured products (e.g., collateralized debt obligations [CDOs],credit derivatives) - See *key terms*

1.3 Demonstrate knowledge of the concept of structures in investments.

For example:

Describe how structures help to distinguish alternative investments from traditional investments

Traditional equities are listed on an exchange while private equity is not.

Define the five primary types of structures

1. **Regulatory structures**: Government's role in influencing the nature of an investment via regulation and taxation.
2. **Securities structures**: The structuring of cash flows through securitization.
3. **Trading structures**: Role of an investment vehicle's investment managers in developing and implementing trading strategies. (e.g. buy-and-hold vs. fast-paced strategy)
4. **Compensation structures**: Describes the fee structures used to compensate managers.
5. **Institutional structures**: Refers to the extent that an investment is held by institutions.

Recognize the primary structures that influence the five alternative asset types

1. **Real assets** – Most real estate has the *institutional* structure of being privately held and traded. Also, the use of securities in the structuring and of cash flows and securitization also important.
2. **Hedge funds** – Primarily driven by the *trading* structure
3. **Commodities** – Primarily driven by their *securities* structure since they are usually traded using futures contracts
4. **Private equity** – Distinguished by *institutional* structure in that it is not publicly traded. Compensation, securities and trading structures also play important roles.
5. **Structured products** –Distinguished by *securities* structure. Also somewhat influenced by institutional, regulatory and compensation structures.

Recognize the limits of using structures to categorize alternative investments

- Some alternative investments (e.g. timber) have minimal influences from structures
- Investments such as equity derivatives and interest rate derivatives can be heavily structured yet considered traditional investments

1.4 Demonstrate knowledge of how alternative and traditional investments are distinguished by return characteristics.

For example:

Recognize the role of absolute return products as diversifiers

Absolute return products have the potential to diversify risk since their returns can be uncorrelated or slightly correlated with traditional investments.

Define illiquidity and describe the advantages and risks of illiquid investments

Illiquidity describes an investment that trades infrequently and/or with low volume.

Advantages: Potential higher returns.

Risks: Thin trading causes a more uncertain relationship between the most recently observed price and the likely price of the next transaction. Illiquid assets can also be difficult to sell due to thin volume or lockup provisions.

Define efficiency and inefficiency and describe their relationship to competition and transactions costs

Efficiency is the tendency of market prices to reflect all available information. Asserts that arbitrage opportunities and superior risk-adjusted returns are more likely to be identified in markets that are less competitively traded and less efficient.

Inefficiency is the deviation of actual valuations from anticipated valuations given an efficient market. Inefficient markets are less competitive, with fewer investors and higher transaction costs. Many alternative investments have the institutional structure of trading at inefficient prices.

Recognize normal and non-normal distributions and the structures that cause non-normality

Over the long-term, the returns of many alternative investments exhibit non-normality in that they cannot be accurately approximated using the standard bell curve.

Structures that cause non-normality:

- Many alternative investments are structured so that they are infrequently traded and so their market returns are measured over longer intervals, making it harder to approximate their returns using a normal distribution
- Securities structuring using derivatives that are nonlinearly related to the underlying securities
- Trading structures that alternate between long and short positions

1.5 Demonstrate knowledge of how alternative and traditional investments are distinguished by methods of analysis.

For example:

Recognize return computation methodologies

- Internal rate of return (IRR)
- In the case of no investment outlay, may utilize other concepts of valuation such as notional principal amounts

Recognize statistical methodologies

- Mean
- Standard deviation / variance

Recognize examples of valuation methodologies

- Traditional investments: fundamental equity valuation models
- Alternative investments: complex statistical models for active trading strategies

Recognize portfolio management methodologies

- Traditional investments: Methods rely on assumptions such as the ability to transact quickly, relatively low transaction costs, and ability to confine an analysis to mean and variance of the portfolio's return.
- Alternative investments: Methods address non-normality of returns – skewness and kurtosis. Liquidity management is more of an issue. Tends to focus more on the potential to generate superior returns.

1.6 Demonstrate knowledge of the goals of alternative investing.

For example:

Define active management and contrast active management and passive investing

Active management describes efforts of buying and selling securities with the intent of earning superior risk-adjusted return. Passive investing describes buying and holding securities to match the risk and return of a benchmark, like an index.

Recognize the importance of benchmarks and benchmark returns in managing investments

Benchmarks enable an investor to judge the efficacy of the investment strategy employed by the manager.

Define active risk and active return

Active risk is the risk that causes a portfolio's return to deviate from the return of a benchmark due to active management. Active return is the difference between the return of a portfolio and its benchmark that is due to active management.

Describe the absolute and relative standards for evaluating returns

Absolute return standard is when returns are evaluated independent of performance in equity or debt markets. Relative return standard is when returns are evaluated relative to a benchmark.

Describe the concept of arbitrage and the roles of return enhancers and return diversifiers in an investment program.

Arbitrage describes the attempt to earn *risk-free* profits through the simultaneous purchase and sale of identical positions trading at different prices in different markets. Adding a return diversifier to a portfolio can reduce the portfolio's risk due to its lack of correlation with the other assets in the portfolio. A return enhancer has superior average returns.

Chapter 2: The Environment of Alternative Investments

Keywords

Bid-ask spread: Difference between the highest bid price (the price an investor receives to sell a security) and the lowest offer/ask (the price an investor pays to purchase a security) price.

Buy-side: Refers to the institutions and entities that buy large quantities of securities for their portfolios.

Call markets: Generally smaller markets that follow a pattern of price setting, a period of negotiation and negotiated price setting, and a set period of trading.

Churning: Excessive trading of a client's account for the purpose of generating commissions.

Commission de Surveillance du Secteur Financier (CSSF): The competent authority for the public auditor oversight and responsible for the financial regulation in Luxembourg. The CSSF is responsible for the supervision of credit institutions, experts in the financial sector, investment companies, pension funds, regulated securities markets and their operators, multilateral trading facilities and payment institutions.

Continuous markets: Allow continuous trading as long as the market is open.

Dark pool: Refers to non-exchange trading by large market participants that is hidden from the view of most market participants.

Data providers: Supply funds mainly with raw data, including security prices, trading information and indices.

Family office: Group of investors joined by familial or other ties that manage their personal investments as a single entity, sometimes hiring professional managers.

Fourth markets: Electronic exchanges that allow traders to quickly buy and sell exchange-listed stocks via an electronic system. Does not formally list stocks.

Management company operating agreement: An agreement between members of an LLC and the conduct of its business related to the law.

Market making: The practice of a market participant that deals securities by selling at the ask price and buying at the bid price, thereby receiving the bid-ask spread as compensation for providing the market with liquidity. Market makers sell to and buy from market takers.

Market orders: Cause immediate execution at the best available prices.

Market takers: Participants that place market orders. They buy at ask prices and sell at bid prices.

Markets in Financial Instruments Directive (MiFID):An EU law that establishes uniform regulation for investment managers in the European Economic Area (EU plus Iceland, Norway and Liechtenstein).

Partnership agreement: Formal written contract that creates a partnership.

Platforms: Systems that provide access to financial markets, portfolio management systems, accounting and reporting systems, and risk management systems.

Primary market: The process of selling new securities to investors directly from the issuer.

Private-placement memoranda: Offering documents describing an alternative investment opportunity.

Regulation T margin rule: Rule that requires a deposit of at least 50% of the purchase cost or short sale proceeds of a trade.

Secondary market: Facilitates trading among investors of previously issued securities.

Section 3(c)1: Exemption that allows hedge funds and other alternative investment pools to typically avoid registration if the number of beneficial owners is limited to 100.

Section 3(c)7: Waives registration for alternative investments if there are no more than 500 super-qualified investors.

Sell-side: Institutions that act as agents for investors when they trade securities (e.g. large dealer banks).

Soft dollar arrangements: Agreement where an investment advisor receives research services from a broker-dealer in exchange for trading commissions paid out of the fund or client account.

Software: May consist of pre-packaged software programs and programming languages.

Subscription agreement: An application submitted by an investor who wants to join a limited partnership.

Systemic risk: Potential for economy-wide or even worldwide losses as a result of potential failures of financial markets, institutions (e.g. banks) or even participants (e.g. funds)

Third markets: Regional exchanges where stocks listed in primary and secondary markets are traded. Segment of the OTC market.

Universal banking: Banks that can engage in both commercial and investment banking.

<u>**Learning Objectives**</u>

2.1 Demonstrate knowledge of participants in the alternative investing environment.

For example:

Identify buy side participants (e.g., plan sponsors; foundations and endowments; home office, private wealth institutions; sovereigns/non-federal government funds; hedge funds; funds of funds; private equity funds; commodity trading advisors; separately managed accounts) and describe their roles in the alternative investing environment

- Plan sponsors: A company or employer that establishes a health care or retirement plan (pension) with special legal or taxation status (e.g. 401k plan). The plan trustee manages that plan's assets.
- Foundations: Nonprofit organization

- Endowments: A fund bestowed upon an individual or institution (e.g. university, hospital) to be used by that entity for a specific purpose.
- Home office, private wealth institutions: Private management advisory firms that serve high net worth investors.
- Sovereigns/non-federal government funds: State-owned investment funds
- Hedge funds: Privately organized investment vehicle that uses its less regulated nature to generate investment opportunities that are substantially distinct from opportunities offered by traditional investment vehicles.
- Funds of funds: Funds that invest in other funds.
- Private equity funds: Funds that invest in stock of nonpublic companies.
- Commodity trading advisors (CTAs): Asset managers who focus on trading in the currency or commodity futures markets.
- Separately managed accounts: Individual investment accounts that are professionally managed. Investors in SMA's own entire shares as opposed to fractional shares in the case of a mutual fund. SMA's can also be tailored to the specific individual investor's objectives.

Identify sell side participants (e.g., large dealer banks, brokers) and describe their roles in the alternative investing environment

- Large dealer banks: Major financial institutions that deal in securities and derivatives. Often engaged in proprietary trading as well as brokering and managing alternative investments.
- Brokers: Retail brokers that receive commissions for executing transactions and that have research departments that make investment recommendations.

Identify outside service providers (e.g., prime brokers, accountants and auditors, attorneys, fund administrators, hedge fund infrastructure, consultants, depositories and custodians, commercial banks) and describe their roles in the alternative investing environment

- Prime brokers: Clears and finances trades for investment manager clients, provides research, arranges financing, and produces portfolio accounting
- Accountants: Prepares fund partnership returns and necessary forms for investors (Schedule K-1).
- Auditors: Performs a year-end audit of the fund
- Attorneys: Helps determine the best legal structure for a fund
- Fund administrators: Responsible for fund bookkeeping, third-party information gathering and securities valuation.
- Hedge fund infrastructure: Includes platforms, software and data providers needed to run hedge funds.
- Consultants: Hired by institutions to provide investment advice, analysis and recommendations.
- Depositories and custodians: Responsible for holding clients' cash and securities and settling their trades.
- Commercial banks: Alternative investment funds may use commercial banks for loans, credit enhancement and lines of credit.

2.2 Demonstrate knowledge of the financial markets involved in alternative investments.

For example:

Define primary capital markets and describe their roles in alternative investments

The Primary market describes the process of selling new securities to investors directly from the issuer. Participants in alternative investments tend to create securities that are not immediately listed. Those participants often use the primary markets as exit strategies (e.g. IPOs).

Define secondary capital markets and describe their roles in alternative investments

The Secondary market facilitates trading among investors of previously issued securities. After an IPO, a security trades in the secondary market. Secondary markets are organized into two types: Floor exchanges and OTC.

Define third, fourth, and private markets and describe their roles in alternative investments

See 'Key Terms'

2.3 Demonstrate knowledge of regulatory issues related to alternative investments.

For example:

Define and explain the concept of systemic risk

See 'Key Terms'

Describe key components of U.S. regulations affecting securities issued to the public (e.g., the Company Act, the Securities Act), including exemptions commonly applied to hedge funds

- Company Act: Refers to the US Investment Company Act of 1940, which deals with the regulation of advisers to investment pools (e.g. mutual funds).
- Securities Act: Refers to the Securities Act of 1933 which governs offers to sell securities issued to the public in the primary market. Alternative investment funds can avoid registration via Section 3(c)1 and Section 3(c)7.

Describe key components of U.S. regulations affecting advisers to investment pools (e.g., the Advisers Act), including exemptions commonly applied to hedge fund managers

- Advisers Act: provides a number of exemptions from the investment adviser registration requirements, including:
  - Advisers solely to VC funds
  - Advisers solely to qualifying private funds with under $150 million in AUM
  - Family offices
  - Foreign private advisers

Describe key components of European regulations affecting hedge funds (e.g., Undertakings for Collective Investment in Transferable Securities [UCITS],Markets in Financial Instruments Directive [MiFID]) and recognize major European regulatory institutions

- Undertakings for Collective Investment in Transferable Securities [UCITS] – a hedge fund-like investment pool that conforms to European regulations such that the product can be sold throughout the various members of the EU.
- MiFID – see 'Key Terms'
- Major European regulatory institutions include:
    - FSA: The primary regulator of investments in the UK
    - Autorites des Marches Financiers (AMF): Regulates hedge funds in France
    - FINMA: Switzerland

Describe key components of hedge fund regulations outside of the United States and European Union (e.g., Australia, Brazil, Canada, Japan, Singapore, South Africa, United Arab Emirates) and recognize major regulatory institutions in these regions

- ASIC: Australia. Does not regulate hedge funds differently from other managed funds.
- CVM: Brazil. Regulates funds through a classification system and controls eligible investors, valuation standards, and reports.
- CAS: Canada. Most hedge funds are distributed as principal protected notes.
- Japanese hedge fund regulations are relatively loose under the Financial Services Agency (FSA)
- MAS: Singapore. Regulation and taxation regimes have been loosened.
- DESA: Dubai. Taxes are generally zero.
- South Africa: Hedge funds cannot be marketed to retail investors and hedge fund products are not regulated.
2.4 Demonstrate knowledge of how taxation affects investments and investment decisions.

For example:

Recognize income tax conventions (e.g., taxes on capital gains, dividends, interest)

- Most major economies tax investment income but offer reduced rates on some or all capital gains, dividends and interest.
- Other jurisdictions have no income tax or at least no income tax on particular investment pools (Cayman Islands, British Virgin Islands, Bermuda, Ireland, Luxembourg, Guernsey, and Mauritius). Investors are taxes only by their home country.

Recognize non-income tax conventions (e.g., real estate tax, estate tax, value-added tax)

- Real estate – usually assessed by local jurisdictions to fund local services (e.g. schools)
- Estate tax – can be very high for wealthy individuals
- Value-added tax (VAT)
    - UK: 0.5% stamp tax on investment transactions
    - France: 19.6% VAT tax on commissions and not the entire transaction value

Analyze how variation in income tax conventions around the world affect investments and investment decisions

- The international convention on taxing income on foreign investments is to make sure that the investor pays taxes to at least one country
- A network of international tax treaties has been signed to prevent double taxation between countries

Chapter 3: Statistical Foundations

Keywords

Arithmetic mean: Arithmetic mean equals the sum of all data divided by the number of observations.

Autoregressive: A stochastic process used in statistical calculations in which future values are estimated based on a weighted sum of past values.

Autocorrelation: Correlations of returns with each other.

Conditional value-at-risk: A risk assessment technique often used to reduce the probability a portfolio will incur large losses. This is performed by assessing the likelihood (at a specific confidence level) that a specific loss will exceed the value at risk. Mathematically speaking, CVaR is derived by taking a weighted average between the value at risk and losses exceeding the value at risk.

Conditionally heteroskedastic: In dealing with conditional expectations of Yt given Xt, the sequence {Yt}t=1n is said to be heteroscedastic if the conditional variance of Yt given Xt, changes with t. Some authors refer to this as conditional heteroscedasticity to emphasize the fact that it is the sequence of conditional variances that changes and not the unconditional variance.

Continuous compounding: Assumes that earnings can instantaneously be reinvested.

Discrete compounding: Earnings are reinvested at specific intervals.

Drawdown: The measure of the decline from a historical peak in some variable (typically the cumulative profit or total open equity of a financial trading strategy).

Ex ante: Expectational return of a probability distribution.

Ex post: Another term for actual returns

Excess kurtosis: Subtracts 3 from the kurtosis formula to measure the level of kurtosis that is higher than observed in a normal distribution (which has a kurtosis of 3)

Formula: Excess Kurtosis $= [\frac{E[(R-\mu)^4]}{\sigma^4} * \frac{n(n+1)}{(n-1)(n-2)(n-3)}] - \frac{3(n-1)^2}{(n-2)(n-3)}$

GARCH: Approach to estimate volatility in financial markets. The general process for a GARCH model involves three steps. The first is to estimate a best-fitting autoregressive model; secondly, compute autocorrelations of the error term and lastly, test for significance.

Geometric mean return: Used to calculate the average rate per period on an investment that is compounded over multiple periods. Similar to calculating the compound annual growth rate, the year-over-year growth rate of an investment over a specified period of time. Always less than or equal to arithmetic mean. Only equal to arithmetic mean if all values are the same.

Heteroskedasticity: Residual variance related to level of independent variables. In the case of heteroskedasticity, the variance of residuals is not the same across all observations and there are subsamples more spread out than rest of the sample.

Histogram: A graphical representation of a frequency distribution.

Homoskedasticity: When the variance of the residual term is constant (the same) for all observations.

Illiquidity: The idea that many alternative investments are thinly traded.

Jarque–Bera test: Test for normality using a test statistic that is a function of relative skewness and excess kurtosis of the sample. If the JB statistic > critical value, then the null hypothesis of normality is rejected using the stated level of confidence.

JB statistic $= (n/6)*[S^2+(K^2/4)]$ where S = the skewness of the sample

Kurtosis: Measures how peaked a distribution is. Kurtosis $= \dfrac{E[(R-\mu)^4]}{\sigma^4} * \dfrac{n(n+1)}{(n-1)(n-2)(n-3)}$

Leptokurtosis: When a return distribution has positive excess kurtosis.

Log returns: Logarithmic returns are often used by academics in their research. The main advantage is that the continuously compounded return (log) is symmetric, while the arithmetic return is not: positive and negative percent arithmetic returns are not equal. This means that an investment of $100 that yields an arithmetic return of 50% followed by an arithmetic return of -50% will result in $75, while an investment of $100 that yields a logarithmic return of 50% followed by a logarithmic return of -50% it will remain $100.

Lognormal: A random variable Y follows lognormal distribution if its natural logarithm is normally distributed (the log is normal). It is bounded below by 0 (like asset prices) and skewed to the right.

Mean: Mean and expected value are used synonymously to refer to one measure of the central tendency either of a probability distribution or of the random variable characterized by that distribution. In the case of a discrete probability distribution of a random variable X, the mean is equal to the sum over every possible value weighted by the probability of that value.

Median: The number that lies in the 50th percentile when the observations are ranked from high to low or low to high.

Mesokurtosis: When a return distribution has no excess kurtosis.

Mode: The most frequent outcome.

Monte Carlo analysis: Generation of large number of random samples from specified probability distributions to represent risk. Also used to develop estimates of VAR and value complex securities (European options, MBS with complex embedded options).

Non-linearity: When the dispersion of returns changes through time even as volatility of the underlying asset remains constant.

Parametric VaR: Called the Parametric VaR because one of its fundamental assumptions is that the return distribution belongs to a family of parametric distributions such as the normal or the lognormal distributions

Platykurtosis: When a return distribution has negative excess kurtosis.

Return computation interval: Smallest time interval for which returns are calculated (e.g. daily, monthly, annually)

Semistandard deviation: The square root of the semivariance.

Semivariance: Focuses entirely on the downside of the return distribution. Computed without outcomes that are above the mean (other than to compute the mean itself).

Shortfall risk: The probability that the return will be less than the investor's target rate of return.

Simple interest: The amount of interest paid based on only the original amount lent or borrowed

Skewness: Numerical measure of the extent to which a distribution flares out in one direction or the other.
$\text{Skewness} = \frac{E[(R-\mu)^3]}{\sigma^3} * [\frac{n}{(n-1)(n-2)}]$

Standard deviation: Square root of variance = $\sqrt{\sigma^2}$

Target semistandard deviation: The square root of the target semivariance.

Target semivariance: Similar to semivariance except that it substitutes the investor's target rate of return in place of the mean return.

Tracking error: Measure of how closely a portfolio follows the index to which it is benchmarked.

Value at risk (VaR): A statistical technique used to measure and quantify the level of financial risk within a firm or investment portfolio over a specific time frame.

Variance: Expected value of the deviations squared. Equals $\frac{\Sigma_i(R_i-\bar{R})^2}{n-1} = \sigma^2$

Volatility: Measure for variation of price of a financial instrument over time. Usually measure by standard deviation.

Learning Objectives

3.1 Demonstrate knowledge of frequency and probability distributions.

For example:

Describe frequency distributions

- A frequency distribution shows the distribution of returns in a table format
- A histogram is just a graphical representation of a frequency distribution.

Describe the characteristics of ex ante and ex post return distributions

- Predictions are usually formed partially or fully through the analysis of ex ante return data

Recognize the importance of the normal distribution in statistical analysis

- Empirical - The normal distribution tends to approximate many distributions observed in nature and/or generated as a result of human actions and interactions
- Theoretical – The more a variable's change results from the summation of a large number of independent causes, the more that variable tends to behave like a normally distributed variable
- Central limit theorem – the idea that a variable will tend toward a normal distribution as the number of independent influences becomes larger

3.2 Demonstrate knowledge of compounding multiple-period returns.

For example:

Define compounding and apply it to model investment returns

- Compounded rate = $(1+\dfrac{r}{m})^{mN}$
- r = annual discount rate; m = #compounding periods per year; N = #years

Describe continuous compounding and logarithmic returns and identify their uses in modeling investment returns

See 'Key Terms'

Contrast continuous compounding and discrete compounding

- Continuously compounded return = $\ln(1+\text{simple return}) = e^{\text{simple return}} - 1$

Define the return computation interval

See 'Key Terms'

Apply return aggregation over different time intervals

- Simple periodic returns require multiplication for aggregation → use the geometric mean return (CAGR)
- Log returns require only addition when they are aggregated → the arithmetic log return can be used

Recognize and apply the concepts of arithmetic log returns and geometric mean returns

- If daily log returns are normally distributed and independent through time, then the log returns of other time intervals (monthly, annually) will also be normally distributed
- The same cannot be said of simple returns

Identify the advantages of using continuous compounding, rather than discrete compounding, when modeling return probability distributions

- Continuous compounding assumes that earnings can instantaneously be reinvested to generate additional earnings
- Modeling the distribution of noncontinuously compounded returns as being normally distributed over a particular time interval (monthly, for example) means that the model will not be valid for any other choice of time interval (daily, weekly, annual, etc.)
- Since the continuously compounded returns for January, February and March are log returns, then the quarterly return over the same period is additive – not the case with simple returns
- Since the normal distribution spans from -∞ to +∞, simple returns cannot be normally distributed since simple returns can only range from -100 to +∞
- Thus, log returns which can span from -∞ to +∞ are a much better approximation for returns than the normal distribution

Describe the characteristics of log normal distributions

- A variable has a log normal distribution if the distribution of the logarithm of the variable is normally distributed
- If the log returns are normally distributed, then the noncontinuously compounded returns (in the form of (1+rate of return) are lognormally distributed

3.3 Demonstrate knowledge of autocorrelation and non-normality in return distributions.

For example:

Define autocorrelation, describe factors that cause and prevent autocorrelation, and describe the effects of autocorrelation on return distributions

- Autocorrelation is the possible correlation of the returns with each other
- Many alternative investments (private equity, private real estate) cannot be rapidly and competitively traded at a low cost
- When reported earnings can be influenced by an investment manager, it is possible that the manager smooths the returns to enhance performance measures
- These factors cause autocorrelation

- Positive autocorrelation, when a positive (negative) return in a previous period is followed by a positive (negative) return in a subsequent period, causes longer-term returns to have disproportionately extreme values relative to shorter-term returns

Describe the effects of illiquidity on return distributions

- Illiquidity of alternative investments refers to the idea that many alternative investments are thinly traded
- Thus, observed market prices might be heavily influenced by the liquidity needs of market participants rather than driven toward an efficient price
- More likely to have extreme outcomes as a result instead of normal distribution

Describe the effects of non-linearity on return distributions

- A short-term call option is an example of an asset with nonlinear returns
- Non-linearity results in asymmetric price changes and a highly nonsymmetric return distribution

3.4 Demonstrate knowledge of moments of return distributions (i.e., mean, variance, skewness, and kurtosis).

For example:

Explain the first four raw moments of return distributions

Raw moments have the simplest formulas and is just the expected value of the variable raised to a particular power

1. nth raw moment = $E(R^n)$
2. $E(R^1) - E(R)$
3. $E(R) = \sum_i prob_i * R_i$
   a. Expected value of a variable = probability weighted average of its outcomes
4. Mean = $\bar{R} = \frac{1}{n} \sum_i R_i$

Explain the central moments of return distributions

- Central moments focus on deviations of the variable from its mean
- Deviations are the value of the variable minus its mean or expected value
- Variance = $\sigma^2 = \sum_i (R_i - \bar{R})^2 * \frac{1}{n-1}$
- Standard deviation = $\sqrt{\sigma^2}$

Explain skewness of return distributions

- Third central moment
- Skewness = $\frac{E[(R-\mu)^3]}{\sigma^3}$
- Provides a numerical measure of the extent to which a distribution flares out in one direction or the other

- A positive value indicates that the right tail is larger (the mass of the distribution is concentrated on the left side)
- A negative value indicates that the left tail is larger (the mass of the distribution is concentrated on the right side)
- A skewness of zero can result from symmetrical distribution (normal distribution)
- Many alternative investments are likely to have more extreme losses than profits and be negatively skewed

Explain kurtosis and excess kurtosis of return distributions

- In the case of a normally distributed variable, estimated kurtosis approaches a value of 3.0
- Excess kurtosis subtracts 3 from the kurtosis calculation. A positive excess kurtosis is a level of kurtosis that is higher than observed in a normally distributed variable
- High values of kurtosis (or positive excess kurtosis) indicates fatter tails and a higher probability of extreme outcomes

3.5 Demonstrate knowledge of methods for computing sample statistics.

For example:

Recognize and apply the mean for a given set of data

- Sample mean = sum of values *divided by* number of observations

Recognize and apply the variance and standard deviation for a given set of data

- Variance = $\sigma^2 = \sum_i (R_i - \bar{R})^2 * \frac{1}{n-1}$
- Standard deviation = $\sqrt{\sigma^2}$

Recognize and apply the relative skewness for a given set of data

- Relative skewness begins with the sum of the deviations cubed (similar to how variance begins with deviations squared)
- Relative skewness = $S_k = \frac{E[(R-\mu)^3]}{\sigma^3} * \left[\frac{n}{(n-1)(n-2)}\right]$
- The second term on the right side of the equation adjusts for the degrees of freedom similar to how *n-1* adjusts for degrees of freedom in the computation of variance
- μ = mean = $\bar{R}$

Recognize and apply the excess kurtosis for a given set of data

See 'Key Terms'

Describe the characteristics of platykurtic, mesokurtic, and leptokurtic distributions

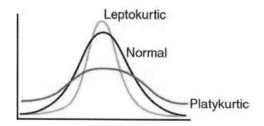

Normal = Mesokurtic

3.6 Demonstrate knowledge of standard deviation (volatility) and variance.

For example:

Define and describe return standard deviation (volatility)

- Standard deviation is the amount by which an investment's actual return deviates from its average

Describe the properties of return variance and standard deviation as they relate to the analysis of investment returns

Variance

- Portfolio variance for three terms: $\sigma^2(R_p) =$

$(w_1)^2*(\sigma_1)^2 \quad + (w_2)^2*(\sigma_2)^2 \quad + (w_3)^2*(\sigma_3)^2 \quad + 2* w_1* w_2* Cov_{1,2} \quad +2* w_1* w_3* Cov_{1,3} \quad +2* w_2* w_3* Cov_{2,3}$

- If the returns between securities are uncorrelated:
  - $\sigma^2(R_p) = \sum_{i=1}^{n} w_i^2 \, Var[R_i]$
- If we assume that the variances of periodic returns are constant (homoskedastic) then the variance of returns for a T-period time interval can be expressed as:
  - $V(R_T) = T * V(R_1)$

Standard deviation

- The standard deviation of a portfolio of perfectly correlated assets is the weighted average of the standard deviations of the assets
  - $\sigma_p = \sum_{i=1}^{n} w_i * \sigma_i$, where $\rho=1$ between all assets
- Standard deviation of levered fund = σ_L = Leverage * σ_u
  - If a fund is levered two to one, then Leverage = 2
  - σ_u = standard deviation of unlevered fund
- Portfolio return = $R_p = wR_m + (1-w)R_f$
  - Where w = weight in the risky asset and (1-w) = weight in risk-free asset
  - R_m = market return
  - R_f = risk-free rate
- Portfolio standard deviation (of portfolio made up of risky and risk-free assets that are uncorrelated) can be expressed as the product of the proportion invested in the risky asset
  - $\sigma_p = w * \sigma_m$
- $\sigma_T = \sigma_1 * \sqrt{T}$
  - A two-period return has $\sqrt{2}$ times the standard deviation of a one-period return

Apply the concepts of return variance and standard deviation to the analysis of investment returns

3.7 Demonstrate knowledge of methods used to test for normality of distributions.

For example:

Discuss tests for normality that use sample moments

- Usually, the true underlying probability distribution of an asset's return can't be observed directly but instead inferred from a sample
- Normal distribution has a skewness = 0 and excess kurtosis = 0
- Normality tests try to determine the probability that the observed skewness and kurtosis would occur if the sample had been drawn from an underlying distribution that was normal

Recognize and apply the Jarque-Bera test

- Tests for normality of underlying distribution
- Perform in 4 steps:
    1. Select a level of statistical confidence
    2. Locate the corresponding critical value
    3. Calculate the JB statistic
        - JBstatistic = $(n/6)*[S^2+(K^2/4)]$
            - where S = the skewness of the sample; and K = excess kurtosis
    4. Compare the JB statistic to the critical value
        - The null hypothesis is that the underlying distribution is normal and that JB = 0 (since the skewness and excess kurtosis of the normal distribution are both zero)
        - If the JB statistic > critical value than the null hypothesis of normality is rejected

3.8 Demonstrate knowledge of alternative measures of financial risk.

For example:

Define and apply the concepts of semivariance and semi-standard deviation

- Semivariance is calculated without using values above the mean
- Semivariance = $\frac{1}{T}\Sigma_t[R_t - E(R)]^2$
    - For all R_t < E(R), or for all values lower than the mean
    - Where T = number of *negative* deviations
- Semi-standard deviation is the squared root of semivariance

Describe shortfall risk, target semivariance, and target semi-standard deviation

See 'Key Terms'

Define and apply the concept of tracking error, and drawdowns

See 'Key Terms'

Define and interpret Value at Risk (VaR) and discuss its strengths and weaknesses as a risk measure

Strengths

- It's a simplified risk measure that can be uniformly computed and interpreted across divisions within a fund or across funds
- VaR is especially useful in situations where a worst-case analysis makes no sense, such as in derivatives, where some positions have unlimited downside risk

Weaknesses

- Provides limited information and can be deceptive
- The VaR can vary widely depending on the statistical confidence chosen

Define and interpret Conditional Value at Risk (CVaR)

- CVaR measures the expected tail loss
- It's the expected loss of the investor, given that VaR has been equaled or exceeded
- It provides the investor with information about the potential magnitudes of losses beyond VaR

3.9 Demonstrate knowledge of methods for estimating value at risk (VaR).

For example:

Apply a parametric approach to estimate VaR with normally distributed returns or with normally distributed underlying factors

Estimating VaR with Normally Distributed Returns

- A parametric approach can be used if the potential losses being analyzed follow a normal distribution
- Parametric VaR = $N * \sigma * \sqrt{Days} *$ Value
    - N = number of standard deviations (2.33 for 99% confidence, 1.65 for 95%)
    - σ = daily standard deviation expressed as a proportion of price
        - a daily standard deviation of 1.35% and an asset price of $20 results in a standard deviation expressed in absolute terms of 1.35% * 20 = $0.27
        - if the standard deviation is expressed as a dollar value of the entire position, then the formula would omit the last term
    - $\sqrt{Days}$ = you use the square root of days because risk as measured by VaR often grows proportionally with the square root of time. (a two-day Var is only $\sqrt{2}$-1 larger than a one-day VaR

Estimating VaR with normally distributed underlying factors

- VaR equation is expressed using the volatilities and correlations of the underlying factors

- The parametric VaR equation can be simple for a single position with value changes that are normally distributed and complex for highly nonlinear portfolios and/or portfolios that depend on several factors

Describe methods for estimating volatility as an input for VaR calculations

- Use the asset's historical standard deviation of returns
- Alternatively, you could use the implied volatilities from option prices

Describe methods for estimating VaR for leptokurtic positions

- Leptokurtic positions have fatter tails than the normal distribution
- As a result, VaR is sensitive to the degree to which the position's actual tails exceed the tails of a normal distribution
- One solution is to use a probability distribution that allows for fatter tails, such as the *t* distribution
- The lognormal distribution is often viewed as providing a more accurate VaR for skewed distribution
- Can also adjust for fat tails by increasing the number of standard deviations in the formula for a given confidence level

Describe methods for estimating VaR directly from historical data

- Can view a large collection of previous price changes and compute the size price change for which the desired percentage of outcomes was lower

Describe the how Monte Carlo analysis can be used to estimate VaR

- A computer can be used to project thousands of scenarios which can then be applied to estimate results in terms of the financial outcomes on the portfolio being analyzed
- These results are then used to form a probability distribution of value changes and estimate a VaR

Discuss the aggregation of portfolio component VaRs to determine the VaR for a portfolio under various assumptions (i.e., perfect correlation, zero correlation, and perfect negative correlation)

- Under perfect correlation, the VaR of the combination is simply the sum of the individual VaRs
- Under zero correlation, the VaR of the combination might be the sum of the individual VaRs divided by the square root of 2
- Under perfect negative correlation, the VaR of the combination would be zero

3.10 Demonstrate knowledge of time series return volatility models.

For example:

Identify various measures used in time series models (e.g., price levels, price variation, risk)

- Time series models are often used to describe the process by which price *levels* move through time

Recognize the key components of the Generalized Autoregressive Conditional Heteroskedasticity (GARCH) method

- The GARCH method allows for heteroskedasticity and can be used when it is believed that risk is changing through time
- The term conditional refers to the lack of predictability of future variation (default-free zero-coupon bonds have somewhat predictable variance)
- When an asset exhibits a clear pattern of return variation (like the default-free zero-coupon bond) its variation is said to be unconditionally heteroskedastic
- However, most financial market prices are conditionally heteroskedastic - they have different levels of return variation even when the conditions are similar (e.g. when viewed at similar price levels)
- Generalized refers to the model's ability to describe wide varieties of behavior (robustness)

Describe how the GARCH method is used to model risk evolution through time

- GARCH can model return variation through time in a way that allows that variation to change based on the variable's past history
- GARCH models are usually specified by two parameters GARCH (p,q) – the first parameter, p, defines the number of time periods for which the past return variations are included and the second, q, defines the number of time periods for which autoregressive terms are included.

Contrast the GARCH method with the Autoregressive Conditional Heteroskedasticity (ARCH) method

- Generalized refers to the model's ability to describe wide varieties of behavior (robustness)
- ARCH allows future variances to rely *only* on past <u>disturbances</u>
- GARCH allows future variances to also depend on past <u>variances</u>

Chapter 4: Risk, Return, and Benchmarking

Keywords

Abstract models: Models that have little or no usefulness in solving real-world challenges.

Applied models: Models that are designed to address real-world challenges and opportunities. For example, Markowitz's model is designed to help accomplish diversification efficiently.

Asset pricing models: Framework for specifying the return or price of an asset based on its risk, future cash flows and payoffs.

Benchmarking: Comparing portfolio performance relative to an index.

Cross-sectional models: Examines data at a specific point in time (e.g. 2003).

Empirical models: Models that are based primarily on observed behavior.

Ex ante models: Models using expected returns

Ex post model: Models using actual returns

Excess return: Refers to the excess or deficiency of an asset's return relative to the risk-free rate.

Fama-French model: Three factors seem to explain asset returns better than just systematic risk, including the excess return on market portfolio (CAPM), relative size (difference between small and large cap stocks) and relative book-to-market value (difference in returns between high book-to-market stocks and low book-to-market stocks).

Fama-French-Carhart model: Extension of the Fama-French model, containing an additional momentum factor (MOM), which is long prior-month winners and short prior-month losers. The idea is that whether a stock has risen or fallen recently helps explain subsequent performance.

Idiosyncratic returns: Returns not due to market correlation.

Idiosyncratic risk: Risks not due to market correlation.

Multifactor models: Models of asset pricing that express systematic risk using multiple factors. They tend to explain systematic returns much better than a single factor model and are generally believed to produce better estimates of idiosyncratic returns.

Normative model: A model that attempts to describe how people and prices ought to behave.

Panel data sets: Observations on multiple phenomena observed over multiple time periods for the same firms or individuals. Time series and cross-sectional data are special cases of panel data that are in one dimension only (one panel member or individual for the former, one time point for the latter).

Peer group: Usually refers to companies that operate in the same industry sector and are of similar size.

Positive model: A model that attempts to describe how people and prices actually behave.

Return attribution: The process of identifying the components of an asset's performance. Also called performance attribution. Benchmarking is one way to perform return attribution by looking at the benchmark return and active return.

Single factor: Asset pricing models that explain systematic risk using just one risk factor (e.g. CAPM).

Systematic returns: Returns due to market correlation.

Systematic risk: Risks (dispersion in economic outcomes) due to market correlation or variation in systematic return.

Theoretical models: Models that describe behavior using deduction and assumptions that reflect well-established underlying behavior. For example, the price of simple options can be deduced through a number of underlying assumptions, including that financial markets are perfect, that stock prices follow a particular process and that arbitrage opportunities do not exist.

Time-series models: Analyze data during a time frame (e.g. 2003-2009).

Learning Objectives

4.1 Demonstrate knowledge of benchmarking and its role in the analysis of risk and return of investments.

For example:

Define benchmarking in the context of investing

- Benchmarking is typically performed by investors and analysts for the purposes of monitoring performance.

Recognize various types of benchmarks (i.e., peer benchmarks and benchmark indices)

- Peer benchmarks are based on the returns of similar companies or a peer group
- Benchmark indices are composed of security returns of a broader market, sector or asset class

Apply the concept of benchmarking

- Benchmarking can be used to calculate a fund's excess return of an index

Examine complexities involved in interpreting the results of benchmark analyses

- The benchmark may not be appropriate
- Did the asset not just outperform the index but to an economically and statistically significant degree?
- Determine the source of outperformance; maybe this was due to different risk exposures

4.2 Demonstrate knowledge of asset pricing models.

For example:

Describe the key components of asset pricing models

- Asset pricing models are focused on returns rather than prices
- Some asset pricing models are single-factor while others are multi-factor

4.3 Demonstrate knowledge of various types of asset pricing models.

For example:

Define normative and positive models and compare their key characteristics

- A normative model like Markowitz's work on diversification describes how people should behave
- A positive model might draw from behavioral economics and finance to incorporate psychological factors that may cause human decisions to differ from rational decisions

Define theoretical and empirical models and compare their key characteristics

- Theoretical models are better at explaining behavior in more simplified situations where the relationships among variables can be somewhat clearly understood through logic. Using the no arbitrage assumption it can be shown with theory how forward rates depend directly on current market prices and interest rates.
- Empirical models are better at explaining complex behavior when there are many observations available and the relative behavior of the variables is fixed or changing in predictable ways. For frequently traded but complex securities, empirical models may simply fit curves to the relationships based on historical data, making theoretical modeling impractical. Alternative investing tends to lend itself more to empirical models than to theoretical models.

Define applied and abstract models and compare their key characteristics

- Markowitz's model provides insight on how to achieve diversification in a portfolio, and is an example of an applied model
- An asset pricing model describing a world with only two people with specific utility functions would be an example of an abstract model
- Models in alternative investing are applied models and are intended and used for solving real-world problems (e.g., managing risk)

Describe the advantages and disadvantages of various types of models in the context of alternative investments

- The CAIA curriculum will focus on applied models although there is some value in studying abstract models

4.4 Demonstrate knowledge of cross-sectional and time-series approaches.

For example:

Define cross-sectional and time-series approaches and compare their key characteristics

See 'Key Terms'

Discuss applications of asset pricing models in cross-sectional and time-series analyses

- Cross-sectional asset pricing models can explain differences in expected or actual returns between securities at the same point in time, in particular, explaining return differences due to risk differences. Cross-sectional analyses are useful in constructing peer group analyses.
- Time series analyses are useful in identifying the factors contributing to an investment product's return and help explain the return volatility of an investment product

4.5 Demonstrate knowledge of single-factor asset pricing models and ex ante pricing.

For example:

Describe the key characteristics of ex ante and ex post asset pricing models

See 'Key Terms'

Recognize the distinctions between ex ante asset pricing and ex post asset pricing

- Ex ante asset pricing uses ex ante models
- Ex ante post pricing uses ex post models

Apply ex ante and ex post pricing for a single-factor model

- Use CAPM
- Ex ante (uses *expected* return measures): $E(R_i) = R_f + \beta_i[E(R_m)-R_f]$
- Ex post (uses *actual* return measures and adds a term that represents the portion of the excess return due to the effect of idiosyncratic risk): $R_i = R_f + \beta_i(R_m-R_f) + \varepsilon_{i,t}$

Define systematic and idiosyncratic risk and return

See 'Key Terms'

Compare the capital asset pricing model (CAPM) with other single-factor models

- CAPM specifically identifies the single factor: the return of the overall market portfolio. It predicts that all risk seeking investors will invest a portion of their portfolios in the market portfolio of all risk y assets.
- Other single factor asset pricing models are primarily empirical. These models assume that securities share a general correlation due to being within the same general economy

4.6 Demonstrate knowledge of the use of the capital asset pricing model (CAPM) in empirical analysis.

For example:

Perform return attribution using the CAPM and interpret the results

- Using CAPM and realized returns, you can solve for $\varepsilon_{i,t}$ (the portion of the excess return due to the effect of idiosyncratic risk)
- This represents the portion of the asset's realized return that is not attributable to market risk
- If this factor is negative, then the realized return should be higher given the level of risk taken

Examine time-series returns with a CAPM-based regression model

- A time series model: $R_{i,t} - R_f = a_i + \beta_i(R_{m,t}-R_f) + \varepsilon_{i,t}$
- Regressed over *t* periods where *a* is the intercept
- The time series model explains the returns of a security or fund through time
- An analyst would use a time series model for estimating the beta of an asset or estimating the potential for an asset to offer superior returns through having an intercept (*a*) with a positive value

Apply CAPM-based benchmarking and interpret the results

- If the intercept (*a*) is positive (e.g. 1.5%), then the asset's performance was 1.5% higher than would be obtained in a perfectly efficient market

Examine and interpret cross-sectional returns with a CAPM-based regression model

- The purpose of cross-sectional analysis is to use attributes specific to each investment, such as historical estimates of its beta risk, to determine the sources of returns
- A typical cross-sectional model: $R_i - R_f = a + B_1 * Beta + B_2 * X_i + \varepsilon_i$
- The purpose of using the above equation in a linear regression would be to determine whether cross-sectional returns can be explained only by beta or whether an additional explanation can be found through another attribute (X_i)

Analyze the strengths and weaknesses of the CAPM model in empirical testing

- Strength of CAPM: simplicity
- Weaknesses of CAPM
  - Realized returns are correlated with total risk (market+idiosyncratic) rather than just market risk as CAPM asserts
  - Hence, multi-factor models are stressed, which are especially important for alternative investments

4.7 Demonstrate knowledge of multi-factor return models.

For example:

Apply and interpret equations representing ex ante and ex post forms of multifactor asset pricing models

- General *ex ante* form of multi-factor model:
  - $E(R_i) - R_f = \sum_{j=1}^{J} \beta_{ij} [E(R_j) - R_f]$
  - Where β_{ij} represents the responsiveness of asset *i* to factor *j*, $E(R_j)$ is the expected return of factor j and J is the number of factors (J>1 for multi-factor models)
- General *ex post* form of multi-factor model:
  - $R_{i,t} - R_f = \sum_{j=1}^{J} \beta_{ij} [R_j - R_f] + \varepsilon_{i,t}$

Distinguish between empirically identified and theoretically derived return factors

- Empirically identified return factors are derived from observation
- Theoretically derived return factors are derived from reasoning based on known facts and relationships

Describe the steps typically involved in empirical modeling of returns

1. R_f is subtracted from the past returns of each security to form the excess return, which is then used as the dependent variable, traditionally located on the left side of the equation
2. A set of potential factors that serve as the independent variables is selected
3. Statistical analysis is used to identify those factors that are significantly correlated with the returns

Recognize the key components of the Fama-French and Fama-French-Carhart models and discuss the appropriate application of these models in alternative investing

- Fama-French model
  - $E(R_i) - R_f = \beta_i [E(R_m)-R_f] + \beta_{1i} [E(R_s-R_b)] + \beta_{2i} [E(R_h-R_l)]$
  - R_s-R_b = The spread of small cap stocks (R_s) over large-cap stocks (R_b)
  - R_h-R_l = The spread of high book to market stocks (R_h) over low book to market stocks (R_l)
- Fama-French-Carhart model: adds a fourth factor (momentum)
  - $E(R_i) - R_f = \beta_i [E(R_m)-R_f] + \beta_{1i} [E(R_s-R_b)] + \beta_{2i} [E(R_h-R_l)] + \beta_{3i} [E(R_w-R_d)]$
  - Where Rw-Rd = the spread between the return of winning stocks (R_w) and declining stocks (R_d) and β_{3i} is the responsiveness of asset i to that spread
- Fama-French and Fama-French-Carhart models are of limited use to alternative asset returns that do not involve public equities

Evaluate various approaches for identifying potential factors

- Inappropriate to test a multitude of potential variables and then find those that are statistically significant since a percentage of those factors will inevitably be statistically significant even if there is no true underlying relationship (spurious correlation)
- Need to identify potential factors using solid theoretical reasoning or rigorous statistical testing

Examine the use of the Fama-French-Carhart model in benchmarking

- Similar to the single-factor model, if the intercept *a* (e.g., 1.5%) is positive, then the performance of the security is 1.5% higher than it would have been had the market been perfectly efficient. However, now other factors other than just the market are included in the analysis.

Discuss the value of ex ante multi-factor asset pricing models in predicting future expected returns

- Although a multi-factor asset pricing model may be successful in explaining past returns, it may not be able to predict future returns

4.8 Demonstrate knowledge of alternative asset benchmarking.

For example:

Evaluate the use of single-period models for multi-period applications with regard to alternative investments

- For CAPM to hold in multi periods, it must be assumed that the market's return process behaves in similar patterns over time.
- Alternative investment returns are dynamic with unusual cash flow patterns and tend to have unusual return distributions introducing a potential issue to the above assumption

Describe the effects of non-normality on alternative investment benchmarking

- Alternative investment returns tend to skew to one side or the other (extremely good or bad returns are more likely than would be expected if the returns were normally distributed)

- Skewness and kurtosis can be so difficult to estimate accurately and can change so rapidly that the meaningfulness of forecasts may be too limited to generate useful results

Describe the effects of illiquidity of returns on alternative investments

- The CAPM idea that investors should seek perfect diversification through holding the market portfolio is predicated on the idea of perfect liquidity – which doesn't apply to alternative investments
- Since most investors are unable to diversify well, they are exposed to risk beyond the market factor, so CAPM may not reflect all sources of risk

Chapter 5: Correlation, Alternative Returns, and Performance Measurement

Keywords

Aggregation of IRRs: Refers to the relationship between the IRRs of individual investments and the IRR of the combined cash flows of the investments (calculating the IRR of one investment versus calculating a combined IRR for a group of investments).

Average tracking error: Refers to the excess of an investment's return relative to its benchmark.

Beta: A measure of the volatility, or systematic risk, of a security or a portfolio in comparison to the market as a whole.

Borrowing type cash flow patterns: Cash flow pattern where the initial cash flow is positive and the remaining cash flows are negative. There is only one IRR that solves the equation. A high IRR is undesirable since the IRR represents the cost of borrowing and not the rate of return.

Carried interest: Share of the profits of an investment or investment fund that is paid to the investment manager in excess of the amount that the manager contributes to the partnership.

Catch-up provision: A clause in the agreement between the general partner and the limited partners of a private equity fund. Once the limited partners have received a certain portion of their expected return, the general partner can then receive a majority of profits until the previously agreed upon profit split is reached

Catch-up rate: The percentage of the profits used to catch up the incentive fee once the hurdle rate is met. A full catch-up rate is 100%. It must be higher than the rate of carried interest in order to be effective.

Clawback clause: A clause in the agreement between the general partner and the limited partners of a private equity fund. The clawback gives limited partners the right to reclaim a portion of disbursements to a general partner for profitable investments based on significant losses from later investments in a portfolio.

Complex cash flow pattern: An investment involving either borrowing or multiple sign changes.

Correlation coefficient: Measure of the strength and direction of the linear relationship between two variables that is defined as the (sample) covariance of the variables divided by the product of their (sample) standard deviations.

Covariance: Measures the linear relationship between two random variables. Unlike the correlation coefficient, covariance is very sensitive to the scale of the two variables.

Deal-by-deal carried interest: Carried interest owed to managers is calculated on a deal-by-deal basis.

Dollar weighted returns: Rate of return that takes cash inflows and outflows into consideration.

First order autocorrelation: Refers to the correlation between the return in time period t and the return in the immediately previous time period.

Fully collateralized: An assumption that the forward contract is assumed to be paired with a quantity of capital equal in value to the notional principal of the contract.

Fund-as-a-whole carried interest: Amount of carried interest owed to managers based on whole portfolio.

Hard hurdle rate: Limits incentive fees to profits *in excess* of the hurdle rate.

Hurdle rate: A return that fund limited partners must receive before general partners begin to receive incentive fees.

Incentive fee: Fund management fee based on the performance of the fund.

Information ratio: Active return divided by active risk.

$$\text{Information ratio} = \frac{E(Rp) - Benchmark\ Return}{Tracking\ error\ of\ the\ portfolio\ relative\ to\ its\ benchmark}$$

The tracking error is the standard deviation of the differences through time of the portfolio's return and the benchmark return.

Interim or Since Inception IRRs: Performance is measured from the start of an investment to a point in time prior to when the investment ceases to exist.

Internal rate of return (IRR): Rate of return used to measure and compare the profitability of investments. The term internal refers to the fact that its calculation does not incorporate environmental factors (e.g., the interest rate or inflation). It is also the rate that makes the net present value of all cash flows (both positive and negative) from a particular investment equal to zero.

Jensen's alpha: Actual portfolio return minus its expected return given its risk as measured by Beta. A direct measure of the absolute amount by which an asset is estimated to outperform, if positive, the return on efficiently priced assets of equal systematic (market) risk in a single-factor market model (although theoretically according to CAPM no asset offers a nonzero alpha).

Jensen's alpha = Portfolio Return − [Risk Free Rate + Portfolio Beta * (Market Return − Risk Free Rate)]

Lifetime IRRs: An IRR that is calculated using all of the investment's cash flows occurring over the entire life of the investment.

M^2 (M-Squared) approach: Expresses the excess return of an investment after its risk has been leveraged or deleveraged to equal the risk (volatility) of the market portfolio.

- $M^2 = [(R_p - R_f)\dfrac{\sigma_m}{\sigma_p}] + R_f$
- Extension of Sharpe – based on total risk
- The first step is to leverage or deleverage the portfolio into a portfolio with the same volatility of the market portfolio
- The most attractive portfolio has the highest M^2
- Determines which portfolios beat the market on a risk-adjusted basis

Management fees: Periodic payment that is paid by investors in a pooled investment fund to the fund's investment adviser for investment and portfolio management services.

Moneyness: Refers to the degree to which an option is in-the-money, near-the-money or out-the-money.

Multiple sign-change cash flow patterns: A cash flow pattern with more than one sign change.

Notional principal: The value of the asset underlying or used as a reference to a derivative position.

Partially collateralized: Describes a position with collateral lower in value than the notional value.

Perfect linear negative correlation: When two assets move in exactly opposite direction (correlation coefficient of -1)

Perfect linear positive correlation: When two assets move in exactly the same direction (correlation coefficient of +1)

Performance-based fee: See Incentive Fee.

Point-to-point IRRs: The initial and terminal cash flows are both appraised values since they occur during the lifetime of the investment (after inception and before termination).

Preferred return: See 'Hurdle Rate'.

Reinvestment assumption: The assumption of the rate that cash flows generated from an investment are reinvested at.

Return on notional principal: Divides economic gain or loss by the notional principal of the contract.

Return on VAR (RoVaR): The expected or average return of an asset divided by a specified VaR.

RoVaR $= \frac{E(Rp)}{VaR}$

Scale differences: Differences in the size and/or timing of investment cash flows. A challenge when comparing IRRs across investments.

Sharpe ratio: Measure of return adjusted for the risk of the investment or portfolio.

Formula: Sharpe Ratio $= \frac{R_p - R_f}{\sigma_p}$ where R_p is the return on the portfolio and R_f is the risk-free rate

Soft hurdle rate: Allows fund managers to earn an incentive fee on *all* profits, given that the hurdle rate has been achieved.

Sortino ratio: Like Sharpe, it is a measure of return adjusted for the risk of the investment or portfolio. Unlike the Sharpe ratio, it penalizes only those returns falling below a user-specified target, or required rate of return, while the Sharpe ratio penalizes both upside and downside volatility equally.

$$\text{Sortino ratio} = \frac{E(Rp) - Target\ rate\ of\ return}{Target\ semistandard\ deviation}$$

Spearman rank correlation: A measure of correlation based on the ranked size of the variables rather than just their absolute size.

Time-weighted returns: Rate of return that eliminates the impact of cash flows. Calculated the same way as the geometric average rate of return.

Treynor ratio: Measure of return adjusted for the risk of the investment or portfolio. Uses systematic risk (Beta) instead of total risk.

Formula: Treynor ratio $= \dfrac{R_p - R_f}{\beta_p}$

Vesting: Process of granting full ownership of conferred rights, such as incentive fees.

Waterfall: Details what amount must be distributed to the limited partners before the fund managers or general partners can take a share from the fund's profits.

Well-diversified portfolios: A portfolio where systematic risk and total risk are equal since all idiosyncratic risk is diversified away.

Learning Objectives

5.1 Demonstrate knowledge of various measures of correlation between assets.

For example:

Recognize the importance of correlation in alternative investment portfolio management

- Correlation affects diversification, which drives the risk of the portfolio

Define and apply the concept of covariance

- Covariance is the expected value of the product of the deviations of the returns of two assets
- The covariance can be estimated from a sample using:
  - $\text{Cov}(R_i, R_j) = \frac{1}{(T-1)} \sum_{t=1}^{T} [(R_{it} - \bar{R}_i)(R_{jt} - \bar{R}_j)]$
- R_{it} = the return of the security in time t
- $\bar{R}$ = sample mean return

Define and apply the concept of the correlation coefficient

- More easily interpreted than the covariance
- $\text{Correlation}_{ij} = \rho_{ij} = \dfrac{cov_{ij}}{\sigma_i \sigma_j}$

Define and apply the Spearman rank correlation coefficient

- Very high or low values can cause the Pearson correlation coefficient to be very near +1 or -1
- Steps
    1. Replace the actual returns with the rank of each asset's return
    2. Calculate the difference in ranks for each time period
    3. Square each difference and add them all together, obtaining Σd_i^2
    4. Use the formula to obtain Spearman correlation: $\rho s = 1 - \frac{6*\Sigma d_i^2}{n(n^2-1)}$

Discuss the role of correlation in portfolio diversification

- There are no diversification benefits if assets are perfectly correlated
- Perfect hedging occurs when two asses are perfectly negatively correlated

Define and apply the concept of beta in the context of the CAPM

- Beta of an asset is the covariance between the asset's returns and an index divided by the variance of the index return
- Beta of an asset $= \beta_i = \frac{Cov(R_m, R_i)}{Var(R_m)}$

Define autocorrelation

- Relationships between the returns of an asset from different time periods
- Also known as serial correlation

Apply the concepts of the first order autocorrelation coefficient

- First order autocorrelation coefficient is the correlation between the return in time period *t* and the return in the immediately previous time period *t-1*
- Because first order autocorrelation is generally less than 1, the autocorrelation between returns diminishes as the time distance between those returns increases

Recognize and apply the Durbin-Watson statistic

- Used to test for the presence of autocorrelation in a time series
- A DW value of 2.0 indicates no significant autocorrelation (fails to reject hypothesis of zero autocorrelation)
- If DW > 2, reject the null hypothesis in favor of negative autocorrelation (usually reject if DW>3)
- If DW < 2, reject the null hypothesis in favor of positive autocorrelation (usually reject if DW<1)

5.2 Demonstrate knowledge of the internal rate of return (IRR) approach to alternative investment analysis.

For example:

Define and apply the IRR

- See 'Key Terms'

Recognize the three types of IRR based on time periods for which cash flows are available (i.e., lifetime, interim, and point-to-point) and their relationship to valuation of alternative investments

- See 'Key Terms'

5.3 Demonstrate knowledge of problems with the use of IRR in alternative investment analysis.

For example:

Recognize complex cash flow patterns and discuss their effect on the computation and interpretation of IRRs

- Complex cash flow patterns involve either multiple sign changes or borrowing type cash flow patterns
- Borrowing type cash flows:
  - Must be interpreted differently
  - A high IRR is undesirable because the IRR is the cost of borrowing
  - An increase in the discount rate *decreases* the present value of the cash outflows
- Multiple sign change cash flow patterns:
  - More than one IRR may exist – all of the IRRs are unusable

Discuss the challenges (e.g., scale differences) of comparing investments based on IRRs

- When comparing investments of different sizes (scale), an investment with a higher IRR may be inferior to an investment with a lower IRR

Discuss the difficulties of aggregating IRRs

- IRRs should NOT be averaged

Recognize factors that contribute to the sensitivity of IRRs to cash flows

- High IRRs are insensitive to distant cash flows but an investment with a large negative IRR is very sensitive to distant cash flows

Discuss the reinvestment assumption inherent in the IRR and how it is addressed by the modified IRR

- The use of IRRs to rank investment alternatives relies on the reinvestment assumption
- The modified IRR approach discounts all cash outflows into a present value using a financing rate, compounds all cash inflows into a future value using an assumed reinvestment rate, and calculates the modified IRR as the discount rate that sets the absolute values of the future value and present value equal to each other

Compare and apply time-weighted and dollar-weighted returns

- See 'Key Terms'

5.4 Demonstrate knowledge of returns based on notional principal.

For example:

Define and apply the concepts of notional principal and full collateralization for forward contracts

- See 'Key Terms'

Apply the concept of the log return to a fully collateralized derivatives position

- The return on a fully collateralized position = $\ln(1+R) + R_f$ where R equals the percentage change in the value of the derivative based on the notional value

Apply the concept of the log return to a partially collateralized derivatives position

- The return on a partially collateralized derivatives position = $[l * \ln(1+R)] + R_f$ where l equals the amount of leverage used (if \$10K of collateral is required for a \$100K position, then l = 100/10 or 10)
- R in this case must be adjusted to reflect the reduced denominator due to the reduced required collateral

5.5 Demonstrate knowledge of the distribution of cash waterfall.

For example:

Explain the distribution of cash waterfall provision of a limited partnership agreement

- A waterfall details what amount must be distributed to the limited partners before the fund managers or general partners can take a share from the fund's profits.

Recognize terminology associated with the cash waterfall provision (e.g., carried interest, hurdle rate, catch-up provision, vesting, clawback clause)

- See 'Key Terms'

Discuss factors (e.g., management fees, incentive-based fees) to consider in a fund's compensation structure and the potential effects of decisions regarding compensation structure

- Compensation schemes should be used to align the interests of the principal (LPs) and the agents (GPs) to the extent that the alignment is cost-effective
- Carried interest tends to be used in private equity and real estate while the term incentive fee is used more often with hedge funds

Contrast and apply fund-as-a-whole carried interest and deal-by-deal carried interest

- See 'Key Terms'

Discuss the concept of clawback provisions, including their purposes and limitations

- The purpose is to make sure that incentive fees paid to management when the firm experiences losses after profits equal the incentive fees paid if the profits and losses occurred *simultaneously*

- Situations arise where LPs are unable to receive clawbacks that they are owed

Compare and apply hard and soft hurdle rates and their sequences of distribution

- Hard hurdle rate:
    - Capital is returned to LPs until their investment is repaid
    - *Profits* are distributed only to LPs until they receive the hurdle rate
    - *Additional* profits are split such that the fund managers receive an incentive fee only on the profits in excess of the hurdle rate
- Soft hurdle rate:
    - Capital is returned to LPs until their investment is repaid
    - *Profits* are distributed only to LPs until they receive the hurdle rate
    - *Additional* profits are split with a high proportion going to the fund managers until the fund managers receive an incentive fee on all of the profits
    - A catch up provision enables fund managers to split additional profits using the incentive fee

Discuss the potential effects of incentive fees on decision making and their option-like nature

- Incentive fees are like long call options to GPs
- If the assets of the fund rise, they receive an increasing payout
- If the assets of the fund remain constant or fall, they receive no incentive fee
- The underlying asset is the fund's net asset value
- The strike price is the hurdle rate (or the NAV in the absence of a hurdle rate)
- When the option is below or near its strike price, the incentive fees incentivize fund managers to take more risk (which increases the value of the call option) since the manager's downside is limited

5.6 Demonstrate knowledge of performance measures used in alternative investment analysis.

For example:

Define the ratio-based performance measure type

- Performance can be measured by using ratios of return to risk or by generating a risk-adjusted return.

*Recognize and apply various **ratio-based performance measures** (i.e., the Sharpe ratio, the Treynor ratio, the Sortino ratio, the Information ratio, and return on VaR)*

- Sharpe ratio
    - Ignores diversification benefits and are primarily useful in comparing returns on a standalone basis
    - Should be used to examine total portfolios
    - Appropriate if examining a well-diversified portfolio (systematic risk = total risk)
    - Sensitive to time dimension – changes significantly if the unit of time changes

- o Less useful in comparing investments with returns that vary by skew and kurtosis (as in the case with many alternative investments) since volatility only provides a partial measure of dispersion
- o The ratio can be manipulated to the benefit of a hedge fund manager using option-like strategies
- Treynor ratio
  - o Unlike the Sharpe ratio, it should not be used on a standalone basis since beta is a measure of only one type of risk (market risk)
  - o Using it on a standalone basis may result in selecting investments that maximize excess return per unit of market risk but not total risk unless each investment was well-diversified
  - o It is designed to compare well-diversified investments and to compare investments that are to be added to a well-diversified portfolio
  - o Less frequently used in alternative investments since beta is not an appropriate risk measure
- Sortino ratio
  - o Tends to be used more in alternative investments
  - o To the extent that a return distribution is nonsymmetrical and that the investor is focused on downside risk, this ratio can be useful
- Information ratio
  - o The use of the ratio is an attempt to drive the portfolio towards investments that track the benchmark return well but consistently outperform the benchmark
- Return on VaR
  - o In cases where VaR is a good summary measure of portfolio risks, RoVaR is a good measure
  - o Such cases include when the risks of the investment share similarly shaped return distributions that are well understood by the analyst

Recognize and apply various risk adjusted performance measures (i.e.,Jensen's alpha, M2 [M-squared], and average tracking error)

- See 'Key Terms'

Chapter 6: Alpha and Beta

Keywords

Abnormal return persistence: The tendency of idiosyncratic performance in one time period to be correlated with idiosyncratic performance in a subsequent time period.

Alpha: Risk-adjusted measure of the so-called active return on an investment. It is the return in excess of the compensation for the risk borne, and thus commonly used to assess active manager performance.

Alpha driver: Describes an investment that seeks high returns independent of the market.

Alternative/cheap beta: Describes any systematic risk that is not common to traditional stocks and bonds (e.g., commodities, real assets)

Asset gathers: Describers large-scale index trackers that produce passive products tied to well-recognized market benchmarks.

Beta creep: When hedge fund strategies pick up more systematic (market) risk over time. This tends to happen as more funds flow to hedge funds and those hedge fund managers take on more beta exposure in their portfolios in an attempt to maintain expected returns in an increasingly competitive and crowded financial market.

Beta driver: Describes an investment that moves in tandem with the overall market.

Beta expansion: The perceived tendency of the systematic risk exposures of a fund or asset to increase due to changes in general economic conditions. It is typically observed in down market cycles and is attributed to increased correlation between the hedge fund's returns and market returns.

Beta nonstationarity: The tendency of the systematic risk of a security, strategy or fund to shift through time. The beta of a firm's equity can shift over time due to changes in leverage through time.

Equity premium puzzle: Lack of consensus among economists on why demand for government bonds - which return much less than stocks - is as high as it is, and even why the demand exists at all. The intuitive notion that stocks are much riskier than bonds is not a sufficient explanation as the magnitude of the disparity between the two returns (the equity risk premium) is so great that it implies an implausibly high level of investor risk aversion.

Equity risk premium: The excess return that an individual stock or the overall stock market provides over a risk-free rate. It is the long-term tendency of beta drivers to earn higher returns on equity than on risk-free investments.

Ex ante alpha: Alpha calculated based on expected returns.

Ex post alpha: Alpha calculated based on actual returns.

Full market cycle: A period of time containing a large representation of market conditions, especially both bull and bear markets.

Model misspecification: Any error in the identification of the variables in a model or any error in identification of the relationships between the variables. Model misspecification inserts errors in the interpretation and estimation of relationships.

Passive beta driver: A strategy that generates returns that follow the up and down movement of the market on a one-to-one basis.

Process drivers: Beta drivers that focus on providing beta that is more and more fine-tuned or differentiated (e.g., beta for a specific market cap or industry).

Product innovators: Describes alpha drivers that create new investment opportunities. Product innovators include the active management segment of the investment industry (130/30 funds, alternative betas, etc.)

Learning Objectives

6.1 Demonstrate knowledge of beta and alpha.

For example:

Recognize the role of beta in the analysis of traditional and alternative investments

- Beta is market risk when analyzing traditional investments
- In alternative investments, beta can be used to refer to any or all systematic risks which cannot be diversified away for which an investor may be rewarded

Recognize the role of alpha in the analysis of traditional and alternative investments

- Alpha can be used to measure the proportion of return attributable to manager skill

6.2 Demonstrate knowledge of the concepts of ex ante and ex post alpha.

For example:

Define and apply the concept of ex ante alpha and identify its key characteristics

- Generated by deliberate over- or under-allocation to mispriced assets and investment management skill

Define and apply the concept of ex post alpha and identify its key characteristics

- Observed in retrospect
- Unlike ex ante alpha, it can be directly estimated

6.3 Demonstrate knowledge of empirical approaches to inferring ex ante alpha from ex post alpha.

For example:

Identify the steps involved in estimating ex ante alpha from historical performance

- $R_{i,t} - R_f = \beta_i (R_{m,t} - R_f) + \varepsilon_{i,t}$
- Alpha is the last term in the above formula ($\varepsilon_{i,t}$)

Discuss challenges to empirical analysis of manager skill

- The distribution may not be normal and the distribution may have contained a higher frequency of extreme outcomes than occurs in a normal distribution
- The sample may over represent successful investors or funds (survivorship bias)

6.4 Demonstrate knowledge of return attribution.

For example:

Identify the primary goal of return attribution

- To distinguish between the effects of systematic risk (beta), the effects of skill (ex ante alpha) and the effects of idiosyncratic risk (luck)

Recognize the key questions to be answered in return attribution analysis

- What was the fund's ex ante alpha?
- What was the fund's ex post alpha?
- What was the portion of the ex post alpha that was luck?
- What was the portion of the ex post alpha that was skill?

Recognize the three primary types of model misspecification (i.e., omitted systematic return factors, misestimated betas, and non-linear risk-return relationships) and their effects on return attribution

- Omitted systematic return factors – Any return attributable to the omitted or misidentified factor is incorrectly attributed to idiosyncratic return, and either skill or luck. If systematic risks have a positive expected return, then omitting a significant risk factor overstates the manager's skill by attributing beta return to alpha.
- Misestimated betas – If beta is overestimated or underestimated, the return attributable to the factors is also overestimated or underestimated.
- Non-linear risk-return relationships – If the true relationship between the return factors and asset returns is nonlinear (as in the case of options) then this introduces error into the identification of the systematic risk component of the asset's return.

Describe various types of beta non-stationarity (i.e., beta creep, beta expansion, and market timing) and their effects on return attribution

- Beta creep – May cause the betas of funds to change due to market conditions rather than changes in the fund's underlying assets.
- Beta expansion – Will also cause the fund's beta to rise due to market conditions
- Market timing – If the manager takes on beta exposure when the market is about to rise and negative beta exposure when the market is about to fall, it is difficult to attribute superior returns to alpha or beta.

Discuss how alpha and beta can become commingled

- Sometimes the line between alpha and beta can be blurred
- In some cases, performance may be related to both

6.5 Demonstrate knowledge of ex ante alpha estimation and persistence.

For example:

Recognize the characteristics of return persistence

- When past performance is related to future results

Define abnormal return persistence

See 'Key Terms'

Discuss attribution of idiosyncratic returns to luck or skill

- This can be done by statistically testing whether the ex post alphas in one period are correlated with the ex post alphas in the time period before

6.6 Demonstrate knowledge of return drivers.

For example:

Discuss return drivers, beta drivers, and alpha drivers

- Return drivers are the investments or strategies that generate the risk and return of a portfolio
- Beta drivers move in tandem with the market
- Alpha drivers seek high returns independent of the market

Discuss the characteristics of beta drivers and their behavior over time

- Beta drivers capture risk premiums by bearing systematic risk
- Bearing beta risk as defined by CAPM has been lucrative over the long run

Discuss passive beta drivers as pure plays on beta

- Passive investing (buy-and-hold) is a pure play on beta: simple, low cost and linear
- The strategy follows the ups and downs of the market on a one-to-one basis

Discuss the characteristics of six broad categories of alpha drivers

- Long/short investing: Goal is to optimize total alpha from both positive and negative bets. They may be market neutral.
- Absolute return strategies: Pursues high returns independent from general market trends rather than relative to an index.
- Market segmentation: Alpha can be affected by decisions to emphasize or avoid particular markets.
- Concentrated portfolios: These portfolios overweight particular markets and frequently have high tracking errors.
- Nonlinear return processes: These functions have option-like payoffs.
- Alternative/cheap beta: Any systematic risk not common to stocks and bonds.

Define process innovators, asset gatherers, and process drivers

- See 'Key Terms'

Chapter 7: Hypothesis Testing in Alternative Investments

Keywords

Alternative hypothesis (Ha): Hypothesis accepted when the null is rejected

Backfill bias: When backfilled data in a database only includes managers with good performance who are more likely to want to publicize their results. Thus, the database investment results are biased upwards.

Backfilling: The act of inserting an investment into a database along with actual trading history for prior periods (generated before the inclusion of the investment in the database).

Backtesting: The use of historical data to test a strategy that is selected after the data is observed. Backtesting with data dredging can generate false indications of future returns.

Bayesian Formula: Calculates updated probability of event given new information.

Causality: When one variable's correlation with another variable is because its value determines the value of the other variable. The rise in the market may cause a long-only fund to rise in value but the long-only fund is probably not causing another long-only fund to rise in value. Their respective rises are caused by the rise in the market.

Cherry picking: Process of extracting only those results that support a certain point of view. An example would be a fund manager only publicizing instances when his strategy worked and not disclosing when it failed.

Confidence level: The probability that a result may *not* be due to randomness. Usually represented as a large probability (90%, 95% or 99%) and equals 100% minus the significance level.

Data dredging: Refers to the overuse and misuse of statistical tests to identify historical patterns. The problem with data dredging is that it fails to take the number of tests performed into account when analyzing the results.

Data mining: The act of repeatedly drilling the same data set until a significant pattern emerges.

Economic significance: The extent to which a variable in an economic model has a meaningful impact on another variable in a practical sense.

Null hypothesis(H₀): The hypothesis to be tested. The null hypothesis is considered true unless hypothesis test gives convincing evidence that the null is false.

Outlier: Values that are unusually large or small. May influence the results of regression and the estimate of the correlation coefficient. Excluding outliers may reduce correlation number.

Overfitting: Small changes in the statistical inputs can cause large changes in the min-var and efficient frontier.

p-Value: Smallest level of significance at which the null hypothesis can be rejected. The smaller the p-value, the stronger the evidence against the null hypothesis and in favor of the alternative hypothesis.

Selection bias: Distortion in the sample selected resulting from the method used to select them.

Self-selection bias: Results in an upward bias when funds that have performed well are more likely to report their results.

Significance level: The probability that a result may be due to randomness. Typically represented as the small probability (1%, 5% or 10%) that a result was falsely generated by randomness.

Spurious correlation: It means that there may appear to be a relationship between two variables when, in fact, there is NO economic explanation for a relationship. Two variables may not be correlated but may show spurious correlation when a third variable is introduced.

Survivorship bias: Upward bias from deletion of the historical performance of funds ceasing to report due to liquidation, failure, or closure.

Test statistic: The variable that is analyzed in order to make a decision whether to reject or fail to reject the null hypothesis.

Type I error: Falsely rejecting a true null.

Type II error: Failing to reject a false null.

Learning Objectives

7.1 Demonstrate knowledge of the four steps of hypothesis testing.

For example:

Identify the four steps of hypothesis testing (i.e., state the hypotheses, formulate an analysis plan, analyze sample data, and interpret results)

1. States a null hypothesis and an alternative hypothesis to be tested
2. Designs a statistical test
3. Analyzes sample data by performing the test
4. Rejects or fails to reject the null based on the results of the analysis

Recognize the components of hypothesis statements (i.e., null hypothesis and alternative hypothesis)

See 'Key Terms'

Describe the process of designing hypothesis tests

- Test statistics are analyzed to decide whether to reject or fail to reject the null
- A confidence level is specified before the test and indicates the probability that a result may be due to randomness. A confidence level of 99% (significance level of 1%) means that there is a 99% probability that the null hypothesis will not be falsely rejected by randomness.

Describe the process of forming test statistics to analyze sample data

- A test statistic is standardized by: $\dfrac{estimated\ value - hypothesized\ value}{standard\ error\ of\ statistic}$
- Creates a test statistic with zero mean and unit standard deviation

Explain the decision-making process for rejecting or failing to reject the null hypothesis

- If the p-value is less than the level of significance → reject the null
- A p-value of 2% indicates that there is only a 2% chance that the estimated value would occur given the assumption that the null hypothesis is true
- A p-value of 2% with a significance level of 5% would reject the null in favor of the alternative

7.2 Demonstrate knowledge of hypothesis testing assuming normality.

For example:

Develop hypotheses based on given information and assumptions

- A typical null hypothesis would be that the expected difference between the fund's return and that of the benchmark is zero
- The alternative could be that the mean is not equal to zero (two-tailed) or greater than zero (one-tailed)

Design hypothesis tests

- Sample null = H_0: $E(R_a) - E(R_{index}) = 0$
- Alternative = H_1: $E(R_a) - E(R_{index}) > 0$

Apply hypothesis tests to sample data

- Calculate test statistic

Interpret results of hypothesis tests (i.e., reject or fail to reject the null hypothesis)

- In this example, if the test statistic < critical value based on level of significance → fail to reject the null

7.3 Demonstrate knowledge of inferential statistics.

For example:

Define statistical significance and recognize common errors in the interpretation of statistical significance

- Outcomes with lower p-values are sometimes interpreted as having stronger relationships than those with lower p-values. But a p-value only indicates whether a relationship exists and not the magnitude of the relationship
- Another error is failing to distinguish between statistical significance and economic significance.
- Another problem is when the level of confidence is interpreted as the probability that a relationship exists.

Recognize Type I and Type II errors in hypothesis testing

- Type I: A false positive or falsely rejecting a true null.
- Type II: A false negative or failing to reject the null when it is false.

7.4 Demonstrate knowledge of sampling and testing problems.

For example:

Recognize the characteristics of unrepresentative datasets (e.g., selection bias, self-selection bias, survivorship bias) and their effects on the interpretation of test results

- When a sample of subsample is a biased representation of the population, then statistical tests may be unreliable

Discuss data mining and data dredging and recognize their effects on the interpretation of test results

- Data dredging may place too much confidence in findings without regard to the number of tests that led to the finding

Discuss backtesting and backfilling and recognize their effects on the interpretation of test results

- Backtesting with data dredging can generate false indications of future returns
- Backfilling revised strategies can provide a biased indication of forward-looking performance

Discuss cherry picking and chumming and recognize their effects on the interpretation of test results

- Chumming is the act of broadcasting a variety of predictions in the hope that some of those predictions turn out to be true

7.5 Demonstrate knowledge of performance reports based on cumulative returns.

For example:

Recognize the characteristics of cumulative return charts and potential errors in their interpretation

- A cumulative return chart graphs the cumulative performance on the vertical axis and time on the horizontal analysis
- A widening gap between the investment and index return can occur if the fund outperformed in an earlier period and that excess return is compounded over time

Recognize the characteristics of cumulative log return charts and how they avoid issues present in cumulative return charts

- A cumulative log return chart graphs the log return (continuously compounded rate) on the vertical axis and time on the horizontal analysis
- In this case, the gap between the fund and the benchmark stays constant

- When the absolute value of a wealth index grows or declines significantly through time, a log chart shows performance adjusted for any distortions from large changes in level → provides a better scale

Examine how erroneous interpretations of cumulative return charts can lead to cherry picking

- Superior performance in early time periods can make it seem like subsequent performance is also superior even when that performance is merely matching a benchmark that has been generating positive returns due to the compounding of the early superior returns
- So, an investment that gets off to a great start can appear to continue to outperform a benchmark
- A fund manager can promote a fund accordingly

7.6 Demonstrate knowledge of statistical issues in analyzing alpha and beta.

For example:

Recognize the effect of non-normality on the cross-sectional search for alpha

- Dispersion from the mean may not be the result of skill (alpha) but from non-normality

Estimate ex ante alpha from ex post alpha and identify potential issues with interpreting alpha estimates and the potential effects of outliers

- Steps to estimate ex ante alpha:
  - Adjust excess returns for systematic risk by performing regressions of asset returns on corresponding risk factors
  - The remaining returns not attributable to risk factors are separated into a mean return that is interpreted as an estimation of ex ante alpha
  - Alpha is estimated using the intercept of a return regression
  - Beta is estimated using the regression coefficients

Discuss the challenges of spurious correlation in the estimation of beta

- Spurious correlation is idiosyncratic in nature, coincidental and limited to a specific set of observations

Compare causality of values with true correlation of values

- Causality is when one variable at least partially determines the other variable

Discuss the effects of data dredging in the context of alpha and beta analysis

- If an analyst is conducting tens of thousands of tests, hundreds or thousands of significant factors could be found even if there is no true correlation
- Data dredging is especially problematic when analysts have prior beliefs or financial stakes in the outcomes

7.7 Demonstrate knowledge of fallacies of alpha and beta estimation.

For example:

Recognize three major fallacies of alpha estimation and the lessons that arise from them

- Funds with statistically better performance are due to manager skill
  - Unexplained returns may be non-normal
  - Even without luck involved, if the skill differentials were normally distributed, only 5% of managers would have statistically higher than average performance
- Statistically positive alpha estimated as the intercept of a regression indicates a higher risk-adjusted return
  - Could be explained by model misspecification
  - The omission of a type of systematic risk factor will cause alpha to contain returns from bearing systematic risk
  - A test is only as reliable of the model itself
- If a statistically significant positive alpha is estimated using a confidence interval of 99% then there is a 99% chance that the investment had positive ex ante alpha, which denotes manager skill
  - The level of confidence is the probability that ordinary performance will be properly judged
  - Only with a well-specified model can it be said that a fund that has zero ex ante alpha has only a 1% chance of being incorrectly estimated as having a nonzero ex ante alpha

Recognize two major fallacies of beta estimation and the lessons that arise from them

- If an analyst tests the relationship between a particular return and a return factor using linear regression, a consistent result that the coefficient is statistically equal to zero means that the investment's return is not related to the return factor
  - Traditional correlation measures only linear relationships and may not catch nonlinear relationships (U or V-shaped)
  - Alternative assets have nonlinear risk exposures and you need more complex statistical techniques
- A statistically significant nonzero beta in a well-specified model indicates that the return factor *causes* at least part of the investment's return
  - Correlation doesn't necessarily equal causation
  - Economic intuition must be used to avoid misinterpretation of spurious correlation

Chapter 8: Land, Infrastructure, and Intangible Real Assets

Keywords

Agency risk: The consequences resulting from one party (the agent) making decisions that are counter to the interests of the owner (principal).

Binomial option pricing: Technique used to price options that assumes that the underlying asset price can only move in a binomial fashion (up or down) during each period.

Blue top lots: An interim stage of lot completion where the rough grading of the property and the lots has been completed. A homebuilder can obtain a building permit at this stage.

Brownfield project: A project with a history of operations and may have converted from a government asset into being privately investable.

Cap rate: Return on asset used to value real estate.

cap rate = discount rate (r) – growth rate (g)

value of real estate = Annual operating income / cap rate

Excludable good: A good that others can be prevented from enjoying due to exclusivity or outright ownership. Many intangible assets are nonexcludable goods especially in the long run.

Favorable mark: A biased indication of the value of a position that is intentionally provided by a subjective source.

Finished lots: Describes lots that are fully completed and ready for home construction and occupancy.

Gates: Restrictions placed on fund withdrawals, such as when investor shares can only redeemed over time rather than when requested.

Greenfield project: A new, yet-to-be-constructed project.

Intangible assets: An asset that is not physical in nature. Corporate intellectual property (items such as patents, trademarks, copyrights, business methodologies), goodwill and brand recognition are all common intangible assets.

Intellectual property: Creations of the mind: inventions, literary and artistic works, and symbols, names, images, and designs used in commerce

Land banking: Aggregating parcels of land for future sale or development.

Managed returns: Returns that are based on values that are reported with an element of managerial discretion.

Market manipulation: Practices intended to mislead market participants through distorted prices or artificially inflated trading volume.

Model manipulation: The process of altering model assumptions and inputs to generate desired values and returns.

Moneyness of an option: The extent to which an option is in the money, at the money or out of the money.

Negative costs: Refers to the costs that are associated with producing a film's negative image. Costs include costs associated with preproduction, as well as actor and crew compensation.

Paper lots: Refers to vacant sites that are approved for development by the local zoning authority but construction has not started.

Political risk: Potentially adverse outcomes due to changes in government policy that may reduce returns associated with farmland ownership.

Privatization: The transfer of ownership of property or businesses from a government to a privately owned entity.

Public-private partnership (PPP): Occurs when a private-sector party is retained to design, build, operate, and/or maintain a public building (e.g., a hospital) often for a lease payment for a period of time.

Real assets: Economic resources that directly generate consumption (e.g., land, infrastructure) .

Regulatory risk: The risk associated with the uncertainty regarding government regulatory actions.

Rotation: Refers to the long growth and investment cycle of timber which can range from 45 to even 80 years.

Selective appraisals: When investment managers choose the illiquid assets that will be appraised during a reporting period in an attempt to manage reported returns.

Smoothing: The reduction in the reported dispersion in a price or return series.

Timberland Investment Management Organizations (TIMOs): Organizations that provide management services that facilitated the migration of timber ownership from long-time corporate manufacturers of timber-related products to institutional investors such as pension plans, endowments, foundations and insurance companies.

Unbundling: The act of isolated intellectual property from corporations so that it can be purchased as a stand-alone asset.

Learning Objectives

8.1 Demonstrate knowledge of land as an alternative asset.

For example:

Identify the three types of land in anticipation of development (i.e., paper lots, blue top lots, and finished lots) and describe their characteristics

- See 'Key Terms'

Discuss investment in undeveloped land as a call option

- The strike price is the cost of developing or improving the land
- The time to expiration is typically unlimited
- The underlying asset is the combination of the land and its improvement or development
- The cost of construction tends to rise with the price of improved real estate (as prices of improved real estate goes up, aggregate demand goes up and the cost of materials & services goes up)
- The payoff of the call option is the spread between the value of the completed project and the cost of constructing the project

Apply the binomial option pricing model approach to valuing land as a call option

Technique that assumes that the price of the underlying asset can only go up or down during each period. Having fixed construction costs increases the volatility of the spread and the option.

Steps to binomial model

1. Use the current price of comparable improved properties and the two possible values of improved properties at the end of the period to determine the risk-neutral probability that the economy will improve
   a. Current value (expected value) = (Up Probability * Up Value) + (Down Probability * Down Value)
   b. Solve for the Up Probability
   c. Down Probability = 1 *minus* Up Probability
2. Insert the calculated probabilities into Equation in 1.a. to compute the value of the call option (the land)
   a. The key is to calculate the amount earned by the developer (value of the improved property *minus* the construction cost) for the Up and Down states
   b. Call option price = (Up Probability * Up Developer Profit) + (Down Probability * Down Developer Profit) = Value of the land

Describe the risks and returns of investing in land and apply the concept of the expected return of land based on the probability of its development

The risks and returns of investing in land:

- Riskier and more speculative compared to other real estate investing

- Lack of revenue and long holding period
- Uncertain prospects
- However, raw land does not deteriorate in value like developed real estate
- Less maintenance

The concept of the expected return of land:

- The expected return depends on its systematic risk (just like a financial call option)
- The expected return is a probability weighted average of the expected return of the *developed* land and the probability weighted average of the expected return of the *undeveloped* land

8.2 Demonstrate knowledge of timber and timberland as alternative assets.

For example:

Describe timber and timberland as investments

- Timber is the investment in existing forest land for long-term harvesting of wood

Describe the risks and returns of timber investment and identify the advantages and disadvantages of timber investment

Pros:
- Low correlation with stocks and bonds (however, this may stem from the difficulty in valuing these illiquid assets)
- Renewable resource with flexibility with timing of its harvesting (timing option)
    - Can time a harvest with income needs or a more favorable price situation
- Variety of uses

Cons:
- Values tied to cyclical industries such as housing
- Long growth cycle (rotation)
    - Pine – 45 to 60 years
    - Hardwoods – 60 to 80 years
    - Cycle can sometimes be shortened to 25 to 35 years

Identify methods of timberland ownership

- Directly owned and privately traded by institutions
- Publicly traded methods to own timber
    - ETFs that track the S&P Timber and Forestry Index
    - REITs that invest in timberland

8.3 Demonstrate knowledge of farmland as an alternative asset.

For example:

Describe farmland as an investment and discuss the characteristics of investing in farmland

- Farmland represents ownership of land but generates current cash flow (crop income)
- Unlike traditional real estate, the annual cash flow is linked to commodity prices rather than rent

- The owner of farmland may lease the land to a local farmer which introduces agency risk
- Must be harvested annually and generally within a window of just a few weeks
- Also subject to political risk (e.g., terminating subsidies)

Recognize and apply the processes for valuing real estate using a cap rate and explain financial analysis of farmland investments

- Return on assets = cap rate = operating income / assets
- Operating income = revenues – taxes – insurance and other operating expenses
- Value of real estate = annual operating income / cap rate

Discuss factors that affect farmland prices and returns

- Macro factors including commodities prices
- Idiosyncratic risks (e.g., poor harvests, cost inefficiencies)

Describe farmland as a multiple use option

- Farmland has multiple uses within and beyond agriculture (residential or industrial development, mineral rights)

Identify methods of obtaining exposure to farmland

- Primary method: Private farmland ownership
- ETFs (DAX Global Agribusiness Index, Thomson-Reuters In-the-Ground Global Agriculture Equity Index)

8.4 Demonstrate knowledge of infrastructure as an alternative asset.

For example:

Discuss infrastructure as an investment and identify the seven elements that help identify investable infrastructure(as different from other assets)

1. Public use
2. Monopolistic power – usually offered by a single provider
3. Government-related – owned, managed or heavily-regulated by government
4. Essential – essential goods like electricity
5. Cash generating – like toll roads (non toll roads are supported by general tax revenues)
6. Conducive to privatization of control
7. Capital intensive with long-term horizons

Recognize the types of infrastructure investments

Economic Infrastructure
- Transport (toll roads, bridges, airports)
- Utilities (electricity)
- Specialty sectors (parking lots)

Social Infrastructure
- Education facilities
- Health care facilities
- Correctional facilities

Discuss the influence of government on infrastructure investments

- Positive: Vast need for new or improved infrastructure assets combined with constrained government fiscal budgets
- The proceeds from infrastructure sales or leases can be used by governments to fund other infrastructure projects or for other fiscal needs
- However, regulatory risk exists

Describe investment vehicles for investing in infrastructure

- Listed stocks & funds, open end funds and closed-end unlisted funds (structured like private equity funds)

Describe the risks and rewards of infrastructure investments

- The least risky infrastructure investments are mature assets with a long history of stable cash flows
- Greenfield investments are the riskiest, especially in emerging markets

8.5 Demonstrate knowledge of intellectual property as an alternative asset.

For example:

Discuss intellectual property as an investment

- An intangible asset that can be owned (e.g., copyright)

Describe characteristics of intellectual property

- Early stage types of IP are like call options with most failing to recoup initial costs but a small number generating large ROI
- Mature IP typically has more certain value

Identify and apply the simplified model for valuing intellectual property

- Based on present value of expected future cash flows
- Value of IP = p $* \frac{CF_1}{r-g}$
- p = probability of generating large positive cash flows
- total annual rate of return = r = p $* \frac{CF_1}{Value\ of\ IP} + g$

8.6 Demonstrate knowledge of the effect of smoothing on the valuation and volatility of real assets investments.

For example:

Discuss the smoothing of prices and returns

- Smoothed reported returns from appraisals can mask risk

Explain the effect of smoothing on observed volatility

- If the highest and lowest returns are smoothed, the observed volatility goes down

Describe ways that values and returns are managed

- Favorable mark, selective appraisals, model manipulation, market manipulation

Discuss how appraisals contribute to smoothing of real asset prices

- Appraisers may inadvertently underprice real assets that experience large upward shifts and overprice those that experience large downward shifts
- Changes in appraised values typically lags changes in actual values

Compare smoothed returns with market returns

- The volatility of returns based on market prices is often higher than those based on appraised values
- Assets that are expected to generate similar streams of earnings should have returns that move together whether they are liquid or illiquid; beware of low measured correlation between these assets

8.7 Demonstrate knowledge of historical performance of timber and farmland.

For example:

Recognize inferences that can be drawn from comparing definable characteristics of timber and farmland investing with their historical standalone and portfolio performance

- Timberland and farmland compared to stock, bond and commodities indices:
    o Lower standard deviation
    o Smaller drawdowns
    o Strong consistent growth
    o Betas and correlations indicate little to no relationship to the market
    o Modest diversification benefits by adding to a portfolio

Chapter 9: Real Estate Fixed-Income Investments

Keywords

Balloon payment: A large scheduled future payment.

Collateralized mortgage obligations (CMOs): CMOs are securities issued against a pool of mortgages for which the cash flows have been allocated to different classes called tranches. Each tranche has a different claim against the assets of the pool and a different mixture of contraction and extension risk. CMOs can be matched to the unique asset/liability needs of investors.

Commercial mortgage loans: Loans that are largely taken out by corporations or other legal entities on commercial properties. The risk of these loans is typically associated with the rental income generated by the property that is in turn used to make the mortgage payments.

Commercial mortgage-backed securities (CMBS): Type of mortgage-backed security backed by mortgages on commercial rather than residential real estate.

Conditional prepayment rate (CPR): Prepayment benchmark for assumed mortgage prepayment rates. CPR is the annual rate at which a mortgage pool balance is assumed to be prepaid during the life of the pool.

Contraction risk: Contraction risk for an MBS refers to undesirable consequences of declining interest rates: (1) MBS exhibit negative convexity (upside is limited due to prepayments), and (2) cash flows must be reinvested at a lower rate. Option-free bonds usually exhibit positive convexity.

Covenants: Terms in debt contracts that either require certain actions of the borrower (affirmative covenants) or restrict certain actions (negative covenants).

Cross-collateral provision: Is used when the collateral from one loan is also utilized as collateral for another loan. Two separate properties may be collateralizing each others' loans. Lenders use this provision to mitigate risk.

Debt service coverage ratio (DSCR): Lenders often use the debt service coverage ratio ($\frac{Net\ Operating\ Income}{total\ debt\ service}$) and the loan-to-value ratio to determine the maximum loan amount on a specific property. A DSCR of less than 1 would mean a negative cash flow. A DSCR of less than 1, say .95, would mean that there is only enough net operating income to cover 95% of annual debt payments.

Default risk: Risk of the borrower failing to make scheduled payments.

Equity REITs: A type of REIT that takes ownership stakes in income-producing property.

Extension risk: Refers to the drop in bond prices and the slowing of prepayments as interest rates increase. Investors would prefer to recapture their principal without a capital loss and reinvest at the current higher rates.

Fixed-rate mortgages: A fully amortized loan with equal monthly payments throughout the life of the loan.

Floating-rate tranches: Tranches that earn interest rates that are linked to an interest rate index (e.g., LIBOR).

Hybrid REITs: Real estate investment trusts that include both equity and mortgage interests.

Idiosyncratic prepayment factors: Factors that are not systematic (e.g., interest rates) that affect prepayment decisions. Option pricing models that assume exercise behavior based solely on interest rates should not be used.

Index rate: A variable interest rate used in the determination of the mortgage's stated interest rate.

Interest coverage ratio: Defined as the property's net operating income *divided by* the loan's interest payments.

Interest rate cap: A limit on interest rate adjustments.

Loan-to-value (LTV) ratio: Financial term used by lenders to express the ratio of a loan to the value of an asset purchased. The term is commonly used by banks and building societies to represent the ratio of the first mortgage lien as a percentage of the total appraised value of real property.

Margin rate: The spread by which the stated mortgage rate is set above the index rate (not referring to the rate charged on margin debt in a brokerage account).

Mortgage: A loan secured by real property through the use of a mortgage note which evidences the existence of the loan and the encumbrance of that realty through the granting of a mortgage which secures the loan.

Mortgage REITs: REITs which invest primarily in mortgages, mortgage securities or in loans that use real estate as collateral.

Mortgage-backed securities (MBS): Security investments in residential or commercial mortgages that are backed by real estate.

Option adjustable-rate mortgage loans (option ARMs): An adjustable rate mortgage that provides borrowers with the flexibility to make one of several possible payments on their mortgage every month. Payment alternatives typically include an interest-only payment, one or more payments based on given amortization periods or a prespecified minimum payment amount.

Prepayment option: The ability of the borrower to make or not make unscheduled principal payments. Can be viewed as a call option on the value of debt or a put option on interest rates.

PSA benchmark: Assumes that the monthly prepayment rate for a mortgage pool increases as the mortgage pool ages (becomes seasoned). The PSA is a benchmark prepayment speed.

Recourse: Describes the potential ability of the lender to take possession of the property in the event of default and the potential ability of the lender to pursue recovery from the borrower's other assets.

REITs (Real estate investment trusts): Tax-advantaged companies that own income-producing real estate. Generate cash flow mainly from lease or rental income.

Residential mortgage loans: Loans that are typically taken out by individual households that do not generate rental income when owner-occupied.

Residential mortgage-backed securities (RMBS): Type of mortgage-backed security backed by mortgages on residential real estate.

Sequential-pay collateralized mortgage obligation: Sequential-pay tranches are a common arrangement for separating mortgage cash flows into classes to create CMOs where each class of bond is retired sequentially. Simplest form of CMO.

Subprime mortgages: Uninsured mortgages with borrowers of relatively high credit risk.

Tranche: A security class that is created, typically with other tranches in the structuring of a CMO.

Unscheduled principal payments: When the borrower makes payments above and beyond the scheduled mortgage principal payments.

Variable-rate mortgages: Loans where the payments are not necessarily constant during the lifetime of the loan as the interest rate is periodically adjusted by the lender.

Learning Objectives

9.1 Demonstrate knowledge of residential mortgages in the context of alternative investments.

For example:

Describe characteristics of fixed rate mortgages

- Fixed rate constant payment, fully amortized
- Equal payments throughout the life of the loan

Identify and apply the formula for valuation of fixed rate mortgages

- Monthly payments can be calculated using the formula for the present value of a constant annuity
- Monthly Payment = Mortgage Balance $* \dfrac{monthly\ interest\ rate}{1-(1+monthly\ interest\ rate)^{-number\ of\ months}}$
- If annual interest rate is 6%, monthly interest rate is 6%/12 or 0.5% (0.005)
- For a 25 year mortgage, n = 300 (25*12)
- Can also use a financial calculator and solve for PMT

Describe characteristics of interest-only mortgages

- Monthly payments are interest only for some initial period
- Most common are 10/20 and 15/15 loans

Identify and apply the formula for valuation of interest-only mortgages

- Interest only payments are equal to the product of the principal balance and monthly rate
- After the interest-only period, the remaining payments are computed like fixed rate mortgages

Describe characteristics of variable-rate mortgages

- Payments are not necessarily constant throughout the life of the loan as the interest rate is periodically adjusted

Identify and apply the formula for valuation of variable-rate mortgages

- Use financial calculator and solve for PMT

Describe other variations of mortgages (i.e., option adjustable rate mortgage loans, and balloon payments)

- See 'Key Terms'

Describe default risk for residential mortgages

- Since most residential mortgages are backed by a public or private entity, investors tend to focus more on interest rate risk rather than default risk
- However, with uninsured, subprime mortgages fundamental analysis must be done to determine the creditworthiness of the borrower and the protection provided by the underlying real estate
- This can be done using ratios
  - debt/income ratio: total housing expenses (principal, interest, taxes, insurance) divided by borrower monthly income
  - front-end ratio: includes only housing costs
  - back-end ratio: includes housing costs plus other debt (credit card, car loans)
  - loan-to-value (LTV) ratio

9.2 Demonstrate knowledge of commercial mortgages in the context of alternative investments.

For example:

Describe characteristics of commercial mortgages

- Backed by commercial real estate
- Usually involve some balloon payment since the loan term is usually shorter than the time required to fully amortize the loan
- Few individuals participate in this market as borrowers or lenders
- Covenants are usually more detailed
- Lender has recourse unlike with residential mortgage loans
- Lenders usually use a cross-collateral provision with commercial real estate

Identify, describe, and apply financial ratios (i.e., Loan-to-Value, Interest Coverage Ratio, and Debt Service Coverage Ratio) employed in analysis of commercial mortgages

- Loan-to-Value: $\frac{amount\ of\ the\ loan}{market\ or\ appraised\ value\ of\ property}$
  - Banks tend to lend at lower LTVs on commercial property than residential
  - Commercial borrowers need a higher down payment than residential borrowers

- Interest Coverage Ratio: $\frac{property\ NOI}{interest\ payments}$
  - Senior secured lenders usually require a ratio of 1.2 to 1.3 (NOI must be 20-30% higher than interest payments)
- Debt Service Coverage Ratio: concerned with all loan payments not just interest (including the amortization of the loan)

Discuss default risk in the context of commercial mortgages

- Defaulting commercial loans are far more likely to be restructured rather than moved into foreclosure

9.3 Demonstrate knowledge of mortgage-backed securities.

For example:

Discuss residential mortgages and their prepayment options

- The borrower can typically make additional and unscheduled principal payments without penalty (in this sense they are callable bonds)
- The lender is short a call option on the value of the loan (put option on mortgage rates)

Discuss and apply methods of measuring unscheduled prepayment rates

- CPR – annualized percentage of mortgage principal repaid in a particular month
- PSA – prepayment benchmark
  - Assumes a prepayment rate of 0.2% for the first month
  - The PCR increases by 0.2% per month for the next 30 months until it reaches a level of 6%
  - The benchmark CPR is then assumed constant at 6% for the remainder of the loan

Describe and apply analysis of residential mortgage-backed securities using Public Securities Association (PSA) rates

- The cash flows of insured residential mortgage pools can be estimated assuming a given PSA speed
- Those cash flows can then be discounted to calculate a present value of the mortgage pool

Identify and describe commercial mortgage-backed securities and compare and contrast them with residential mortgage-backed securities

- CMBS provides a lower degree of prepayment risk than residential mortgages because commercial mortgages are usually set for a shorter term
- In addition, commercial mortgages usually charge a prepayment penalty
- CMBS are more subject to credit risk because they are not standardized making default risks difficult to determine

9.4 Demonstrate knowledge of collateralized mortgage obligations (CMOs).

For example:

Describe the general characteristics of CMOs

- Divides mortgage pool cash flows and distribute them via different classes of securities (tranches)

Identify and describe sequential-pay CMOs

- Simplest form of CMO
- Senior tranches receive principal payments first

Apply sequential-pay structuring of tranches

- Two tranches will both receive their corresponding interest payments in a given month according to their principal balances and coupon rate
- The senior tranche only will receive principal payments until it is completely paid off before the junior tranche will receive any principal payments

Identify and describe other types of CMO structures and tranches (i.e., Planned Amortization Class, Targeted Amortization Class, Principal-only CMO, and Floating-rate)

- Planned Amortization Class
  - More complex structure and riskier than sequential pay structure
  - A tranche may have a high priority to receiving principal payments in one range of prepayment speeds and a low priority under different prepayment speeds
- Targeted Amortization Class
  - Similar to PAC with even narrower and more complex set of ranges
- Principal-only (and Interest-only) CMO
  - PO bonds are paid as borrowers pay principal; bought at a discount from face value and eventually receive face value from scheduled principal payments and prepayments; exposed to extension risk – value declines when prepayments slow
  - IO bonds are paid as borrowers pay interest; cash flows decline as principal is paid down. Exposed to contraction risk since their value declines when prepayments accelerate
- Floating-rate - Adjustable-rate mortgages with interest rates linked to interest rate index like LIBOR

Discuss the financial crisis of 1994 involving CMOs

- Involved CMOs on uninsured residential mortgages
- Interest rates rose dramatically, causing most tranches to extend in maturity as prepayment rates fell
- This caused the present value of most tranches to fall

Discuss commercial CMOs and their default risk

- Primary risk is default risk
- Credit ratings vary considerably between tranches

9.5 Demonstrate knowledge of real estate investment trusts (REITs).

For example:

Identify and describe types of REITs and the potential advantages they offer to investors

- Mortgage REITs: invest in real estate debt
- Equity REITs: invest mainly in equity ownership within the private real estate market
- Hybrid REITs: invest in both markets

9.6 Demonstrate knowledge of historical performance of mortgage REITs.

For example:

Recognize inferences that can be drawn from comparing definable characteristics of mortgage REITs with their historical stand-alone and portfolio performance

- High average returns but large standard deviation, large maximum loss, huge drawdown, negative skew and leptokurtosis

Chapter 10: Real Estate Equity Investments

Keywords

After-tax approach: When cash flows are computed on an after-tax basis and the discount rate is tax-adjusted.

Appraisals: A professional estimate of the value of a real estate property.

Arbitraging stale prices: The act of exploiting stale prices by selling when market prices are artificially high (due to the lag) and buying when prices are artificially low.

Backward induction: Process (in a decision tree) of working from the final decision nodes toward the first decision node, based on valuation analysis at each decision node.

Business risk: The risk that investors may incur a loss as a result of changes in general economic conditions. A property with a well-diversified tenant population is likely to be less subject to business risk.

Closed-end real estate mutual funds: Mutual funds that trade on an exchange with a fixed number of shares outstanding (with real estate as the underlying asset). Shares cannot be obtained from or redeemed by the investment company (unlike open-end funds).

Commingled real estate funds: Type of private equity real estate fund that is a pool of investment capital raised from private placements that are commingled to purchase commercial properties.

Comparable sale prices: Data on the prices at which real estate has traded for similar properties.

Data smoothing: When the prices used in computing the return series have been dampened relative to the volatility of the true but unobservable underlying prices. This act serves to underestimate the volatility of the true return.

Decision node: A point in a decision tree at which a decision must be made by the holder of the option.

Depreciation: The allocation of the cost of assets to periods in which the assets are used (depreciation with the matching principle). A noncash expense that is deducted from revenues in computing income.

Depreciation tax shield: The stream of reduced taxable income due to depreciation.

Discounted cash flow (DCF) method: Under the DCF method, the future cash flows, including the capital expenditures and terminal value, are projected over the holding period and discounted to present at the discount rate. Future growth of NOI is explicit to the DCF method. Choosing the appropriate discount rate and terminal cap rate are crucial as small differences in the rates can significantly affect value.

Effective gross income: Potential gross income minus potential vacancy losses.

Effective tax rate: Actual tax rate paid after factoring in exemptions, penalties and timing of cash flows.

Equity residual approach: Approach to valuing the equity in a real estate investment by subtracting the interest expense and other cash outflows due to mortgage holders (e.g., interest, principal) from NOI and discounting the remaining (or residual) cash flows using a required rate of return reflective of a leveraged investment.

Exchange-traded funds (ETF): An investment fund traded on stock exchanges, much like stocks.

Financial risk: Risk associated with financing used. This risk increases as leverage increases.

Fixed expenses: Operating expenses that do not change with the occupancy of the property.

FTSE NAREIT Composite Index: Consists of a family of REIT performance indices that covers the different sectors of the US commercial real estate space.

Gearing: The use of leverage in investing.

Hedonic price index: Housing price index that takes into account of the quality differences between houses. Hedonic methods which express house prices as a function of a vector of characteristics (such as number of bedrooms and bathrooms, land area and location) are particularly useful for this purpose.

Income approach: The DCF approach (where NOI is discounted at the required rate of return) to valuing real estate.

Inflation risk: The risk that the real value of investment holdings will decrease because of the effects of unanticipated inflation.

Information node: A point in a decision tree at which new information arrives.

Legal risks: Risks from the uncertainty of legal events such as securing and maintaining a clear claim to a real asset.

Liquidity risk: Risk associated with the inability to sell a property on a timely basis and at a competitive price.

Loan-to-value (LTV) ratio: The percentage of a fund's capital that is financed by debt *divided by* the percentage of all long-term financing (debt plus equity).

Management/Operational risk: Risk of management ineffectiveness due to a lack of management skill.

NCREIF property index (NPI): Quarterly time series composite total rate of return measure of investment performance of a very large pool of individual commercial real estate properties acquired in the private market for investment purposes only.

Net lease: A lease where the tenant is responsible for almost all operating expenses.

Net operating income (NOI): Net operating income (NOI) is equal to potential gross income (rental income fully leased plus other income) less vacancy and collection losses and operating expenses (fixed & variable).

Net sale proceeds (NSP): The expected selling price of an investment *minus* selling expenses.

Open-end real estate mutual funds: Public investments that are a non-exchange-traded way to invest in the private real estate market (e.g., mutual fund).

Operating expenses: Fixed and variable expenses associated with the property.

Potential gross income: Real estate rental income if fully leased.

Pre-tax approach: When cash flows are computed on a pre-tax basis and the discount rate is not tax-adjusted.

Private equity real estate funds: Privately organized funds that invest in real estate.

Profit approach:

Real estate development projects: Projects that include one or more stages of creating or improving a real estate project, including the acquisition of raw land, the construction of improvements, and the renovation of existing facilities.

Real estate joint ventures: Private equity real estate funds that consist of the combination of two or more parties, typically represented by a small number of individual or institutional investors.

Real estate valuation: Process of estimating the market value of a property.

Real option: An option on a real asset (e.g., a call option to buy a real asset, a put option to sell a real asset). Real options allow managers to make future decisions that change the value of capital budgeting decisions made today. Real options always add to NPV.

Risk premium approach: Method used to estimate the discount rate by adding risk premiums (e.g., liquidity, risk) to the risk-free rate.

Stale pricing: The use of prices that lag changes in true market prices.

Syndications: Private equity real estate funds formed by a group of investors who retain a real estate expert with the intention of undertaking a particular real estate project. Syndicates may operate as REITs, as a corporation or as a limited or general partnership.

Vacancy loss rate: Rate of potential vacancies applied to the potential gross income.

Variable expenses: Operating expenses that change as the level of occupancy varies.

Learning Objectives

10.1 Demonstrate knowledge of real estate development in the context of alternative investments.

For example:

Describe the processes of developing real estate

- The acquisition of land or a site
- Estimation of the marketing potential and profitability of the development project
- Development of a building program and design
- Procurement of the necessary public approvals and permitting
- Raising financing
- Building the structure
- Leasing, managing and maybe eventually selling the property

Identify and describe the valuing of real estate development as a string of real options (an option on a real asset)

- The real option may be a call option to buy a real asset, a put option to sell it or an exchange option involving exchange of nonfinancial assets
- Each expenditure in the development process may be viewed as a purchase of a call option

Describe and explain decision trees

- Models two types of events: the arrival of new information and decisions
- Information nodes represent a point at which new information arrives

Discuss and apply backward induction using a decision tree

- The process of working from the final decision nodes to the first decision nodes (thus the term *backward* induction) to arrive at a value for the real option

10.2 Demonstrate knowledge of valuation and risks of real estate equity.

For example:

Apply decision trees to the valuation of a real estate development project

- Use backward induction

Recognize and apply the discounted cash flow approach (i.e., income approach) to valuing real estate

- Discount NOI to present
  - NOI = (Potential gross income – vacancy loss) – fixed expenses – variable expenses
  - NOI = Effective gross income – operating expenses
- Discount net sales proceeds at the end of the period to the present
- Can use a risk premium approach to calculate a discount rate
  - $r = [(1+R_f)*(1+R_{LP})*(1+R_{RP})] - 1 \approx R_f + R_{LP} + R_{RP}$
  - R_{LP} = liquidity premium
  - R_{RP} = risk premium

Discuss the use of comparable sale prices for valuing real estate

- Appropriate for non-income producing properties
- Not a viable method when the number of recent and relevant real estate transactions is very limited

Identify and describe the risks of real estate as an investment

- Business risk, financial risk, liquidity risk, inflation risk

10.3 Demonstrate knowledge of alternative real estate investment vehicles.

For example:

Identify and describe private equity real estate funds

- See 'Key Terms'

Identify and describe commingled real estate funds

- See 'Key Terms'

Identify and describe syndications

- See 'Key Terms'

Identify and describe joint ventures

- See 'Key Terms'

Identify and describe limited partnerships

- Fund's sponsors act as the general partner and act as agents of the fund
- Institutional investors such as endowments, HNW individuals and pension funds serve as limited partners whose liability is limited to the equity capital invested into the fund

Identify and describe open-end real estate mutual funds

- See 'Key Terms'

Discuss options and futures on real estate indices

- The payoff of the derivative is linked to the performance of a real estate return index
- Allows investors to gain exposure to the real estate sector without buying real estate properties
- However, the indices underlying the derivatives may not be highly correlated to the risk exposures faced by market participants

Identify and describe exchange-traded funds based on real estate indices

- They may track a real estate index such as the Dow Jones US Real Estate Index
- Since REITs are publicly traded, the use of ETFs on REITs may offer cost-effective diversification but may not offer substantially distinct hedging or speculation opportunities

Identify and describe closed-end real estate mutual funds

- See 'Key Terms'

Discuss equity real estate investment trusts

- REITs with at least 75% of holdings in equity claims on real estate rather than mortgage claims (as in mortgage REITs)
- It uses pooled capital from investors to buy real property directly
- It also manages, renovates and develops real estate properties

10.4 Demonstrate knowledge of depreciation of real estate.

For example:

Describe and apply various methods of depreciation of real estate

- Without income taxation
  - o If the assets earn 10% above and beyond depreciation each year, IRR will be 10%
- With depreciation disallowed for tax purposes
  - o After-tax returns when depreciation is not allowed
  - o By disallowing a deduction for depreciation, the investor is paying taxes before they are due
- With economic depreciation allowed for tax purposes
  - o Accounting depreciation is set to match the true economic depreciation
  - o In this case, the after-tax return generally equals the pre-tax return reduced by the stated income tax rate
  - o The rate of depreciation changes the timing of taxes rather than the aggregated taxable income
- With accelerated depreciation allowed for tax purposes
  - o Defers income taxes and enhances the value of the property thereby increasing IRR
  - o Effective tax rate < stated tax rate
- With expensing of capital expenditures for tax purposes
  - o The initial purchase price is expensed
  - o Generally allowed for smaller and shorter-term assets rather than real estate
  - o Instantly causes the after-tax IRR to equal the pre-tax IRR

10.5 Demonstrate knowledge of real estate equity risks and returns as represented by real estate indices.

For example:

Discuss real estate indices based on appraisals

- Real estate values can be appraised and used as a basis for an index
- Example: NCREIF Property Index

Identify and describe data smoothing, its explanations, and its major effects

- See 'Key Terms'

Discuss real estate indices based on adjusted privately traded prices

- Uses sales prices of properties that do turn over to estimate the value of properties that do not turn over
- The infrequent observation of market transactions can cause observed price changes to lag true price changes in both bull and bear markets

Discuss real estate indices based on market prices

- Uses the reported returns on REITs and are based on observations of frequent market prices
- However, there is a concern that these exchange traded REITs are more correlated to the equity stock market rather than the underlying private real estate market

10.6 Demonstrate knowledge of historical performance of equity REITs.

For example:

Recognize inferences that can be drawn from comparing definable characteristics of equity REITs with their historical stand-alone and portfolio performance

- High average returns but high standard deviation
- 2000-2010 show extreme outcomes not likely outcomes
- Modest diversification benefits based on correlation

Topic 4: Hedge Funds

Chapter 11: Introduction to Hedge Funds

Keywords

Accredited investor standard: The term generally includes wealthy individuals and organizations such as banks, insurance companies, significant charities, some corporations, endowments, and retirement plans. In the United States, for an individual to be considered an accredited investor, he or she must have a net worth of at least one million US dollars, not including the value of one's primary residence or have income at least $200,000 each year for the last two years (or $300,000 together with his or her spouse if married) and have the expectation to make the same amount this year.

Annuity view of hedge fund fees: The prospective income stream of cash flows from fees to a hedge fund manager.

Classification of hedge fund strategies: Organized grouping and labeling of hedge fund strategies (e.g., macro, event-driven, relative value, etc.)

Closet indexer: A portfolio strategy used by some portfolio managers to achieve returns similar to those of their benchmark index, without exactly replicating the index.

Consolidation: An increase in the proportion of a market represented by a small number of participants.

Excessive conservatism: Inappropriately high risk aversion by the hedge fund manager since the manager's income and wealth may be tied to the performance of the fund.

Fund mortality: When hedge funds liquidate or cease operations.

Fund of funds: Funds with a portfolio of other investment funds rather than investing directly in stocks, bonds or other securities.

Hedge Fund: Private, actively managed investment funds.

High-water mark (HWM): The high-water mark ensures that the manager does not get paid large sums for poor performance. So if the manager loses money over a period, he or she must get the fund above the high watermark before receiving a performance bonus. For example, say after reaching its peak a fund loses $100,000 in year one, and then makes $250,000 in year two. The manager therefore not only reached the high-water mark but exceeded it by $150,000 ($250,000 - $100,000), which is the amount on which the manager gets paid the bonus (not the whole $250K).

Incentive fee option: The idea that hedge fund incentive fees can be viewed as a call option on a portion of the profits that the hedge fund manager earns for investors. The call option is on the fund's NAV with a strike price equal to the HWM and an expiration date equal to the end of the period to which the incentive fee applies.

Lock-in effect: The major explanation for the lower tax collections at higher tax rates. The idea is that investors are highly sensitive to the rate of capital gains tax when determining whether to sell stock holdings and other assets. The realizations of capital gains decline when tax rates on gains are increased. When the capital gains tax rate is low, investors are more likely to sell their assets.

Managerial coinvesting: Agreement that hedge fund managers will invest their own money in the fund.

Managing returns: Efforts by fund managers to change reported investment returns toward preferred targets using accounting decisions or investment changes.

Massaging returns: Efforts by fund managers to change reported investment returns toward preferred targets using accounting decisions or investment changes.

Multi-strategy fund: Fund that allocates capital among multiple strategies falling within several traditional hedge fund disciplines.

Optimal contracting: Attempts to align the interests of hedge fund managers and investors with marginal benefits that exceed marginal costs.

Option view of incentive fees: The ability of fund managers to increase the present value of their fees by increasing the volatility of the fund's assets.

Perverse incentive: An incentive that motivates the receiver of the incentive to work in opposition to the interests of the provider of the incentive.

Pure asset gatherer: Manager focused mainly on increasing fund AUM.

Qualified purchaser standard: Requires that individual hedge fund investors have a net worth exceeding $5 million, while institutional investors require a net worth exceeding $25 million.

Safe harbor: An area that is explicitly protected by one set of regulations from another set of regulations. For example, in the US hedge funds are exempt from disclosure requirements of the Investment Company Act of 1940 through one of two safe harbors that are available to funds that do not market directly to the public.

Single-manager hedge fund: Hedge fund managed by a single investment manager.

Learning Objectives

11.1 Demonstrate knowledge of the distinguishing features of hedge funds and their growth and concentration over time.

For example:

Identify and describe the three primary elements of hedge funds

- Privately organized
- Incorporates performance-based fees to managers
- Can use leverage and establish short positions

Recognize and explain the reasons for hedge fund industry growth and concentration

Reasons for growth

- Low correlation with traditional investments
- Investment flexibility
- Potential to generate double-digit returns

Reasons for concentration

- Investors are looking to invest with stable firms with demonstrated risk management processes and risk controls
- Facilitating investor due diligence has become a large expense and is difficult to accomplish for smaller funds

11.2 Demonstrate knowledge of various types of hedge funds.

For example:

Recognize and describe the CAIA classification of hedge fund strategies

- Macro and Managed Futures
- Event driven
  - Activists
  - Merger arbitrage
  - Distressed
  - Event-driven multistrategy
- Relative value
  - Convertible arbitrage
  - Volatility arbitrage
  - Fixed-income arbitrage
  - Relative value multistrategy
- Equity
  - Long short
  - Market neutral
  - Short selling
  - 130-30 funds
- Funds of funds

Contrast single-manager hedge funds, funds of funds, and multi-strategy funds

- See 'Key Terms'

11.3 Demonstrate knowledge of hedge fund fees.

For example:

Recognize and apply the approach for determining total annual hedge fund fees

- Annual fee = management fee + {Max[0, Incentive fee*(Gross return above high water mark – management fee – hurdle rate)]}
- Ending fund NAV = beginning NAV minus management and incentive fees

Describe the effects of high water marks (HWM) and hurdle rates on hedge fund fees over time

- HWMs are used to prevent incentive fees from being paid on recouped losses
- Saves investors money (fees) over time

Discuss the potential effects of incentive fees on hedge fund manager behavior

- Incentive fees can incentivize a hedge fund manager to take more risk, particularly after a period of losses

Recognize and apply the annuity view of hedge funds fees

- The ability to earn consistent (annuity-like) management fees offers managers the highest long-run benefits
- Thus, managers are incentivized to avoid poor returns, retain investors and attract new investors

Recognize and apply the option view of incentive fees and its implications on manager behavior

- Hedge fund incentive fees can be viewed as a call option on a portion of the profits that the hedge fund manager earns for investors

Describe the empirical evidence regarding hedge fund fees and managerial behavior

- Hodder and Jackwerth found that hedge fund managers have an enormous incentive to take on risk depending on the value of the incentive "option"
- When the incentive option is far into the money, managers have an incentive to lower risk to preserve fees (lock-in effect)
- As fund values decline and the incentive fee option becomes far out of the money, the payoff to managers is skewed to the right and risk taking is encouraged
- Also, as the fund NAV continues to decline, there is a point at which it is optimal for a fund manager to close the fund and pursue other opportunities

Chapter 12: Hedge Fund Returns and Asset Allocation

Keywords

Absolute return: Unlike traditional asset managers, who try to track and outperform a benchmark (a reference index such as the Dow Jones and S&P500), hedge fund managers employ different strategies in order to produce a positive return regardless of the direction and the fluctuations of capital markets

Absolute return strategies: Hedge fund strategy that seeks to minimize market risk and total risk.

Backfill bias: Backfilled data in database only includes managers with good performance.

Capacity: The limit on the quantity of capital that can be deployed without substantially impaired performance.

Directional strategies: Directional investment strategies utilize market movements, trends, or inconsistencies when picking stocks across a variety of markets.

Diversified strategies: Hedge fund strategy that seeks to diversify across a number of different investment themes.

Event risk strategies: Directional investment strategies utilize market movements, trends, or inconsistencies when picking stocks across a variety of markets. Computer models can be used, or fund managers will identify and select investments. These types of strategies have a greater exposure to the fluctuations of the overall market than do market neutral strategies.

Fee bias: When index returns overstate what a new investor can obtain in the hedge fund marketplace because the fees used to estimate index returns are lower than the typical fees that a new investor would pay.

Headline risk: The possibility that a news story will adversely affect a stock's price. Headline risk can also impact the performance of the stock market as a whole. Headline risk deters some investors from allocating to hedge funds as an asset class when hedge fund managers make unfavorable headlines.

Hedge fund program: The processes and procedures for the construction, monitoring and maintenance of a portfolio of hedge funds.

Hybrid hedge funds: Hedge funds that combine major asset classes, for example, traditional private equity and public equity within one investment strategy.

Instant history bias: aka "backfill bias". An inaccuracy in the appearance of investment fund returns that occurs when only new, successful funds report their numbers while new, unsuccessful funds close and their poor returns aren't factored into an investment manager's or investment type's overall performance record.

Investability: The extent to which market participants can invest in an index to actually achieve the returns of the index.

Liquidation bias: When an index disproportionately reflects the characteristics of funds that are not near liquidation.

Off-balance-sheet risk: A risk exposure that is not explicitly reflected in the financial statements.

Opportunistic: The strategy is driven by the identification of potentially aggressive exposure to investments that appear to offer superior returns, typically on a temporary (not long-term) basis.

Participation bias: May occur for a successful hedge fund manager who closes a fund and stops reporting results because the fund no longer needs to attract new capital.

Relative return: When an investment's returns are significantly driven by broad market returns and should be compared relative to broad market returns.

Representativeness: The extent to which a sample is similar to the characteristics of the universe from which it was selected.

Selection bias: When certain assets are excluded from the analysis thereby skewing the results. In the hedge fund industry, this can happen when databases disproportionately represent those funds that have characteristics that make reporting more desirable. Thus, bad or undesirable funds are not included.

Short volatility exposures: Any risk exposure that causes losses when asset return volatilities increase.

Strategy definitions: The method of grouping similar hedge funds.

Style drift: Consistent movement through time in the primary style or strategy being implemented by the fund.

Survivorship bias: Funds or companies no longer in business do not appear in data set thus skewing the data.

Synthetic hedge funds: Funds that attempt to mimic hedge fund returns using listed securities and mathematical models. These funds replicate hedge fund returns at a lower cost to investors via lower fees.

Learning Objectives

12.1 Demonstrate knowledge of the hedge fund universe.

For example:

Describe the effect of diversification on performance measures of hedge fund portfolios relative to individual funds

- Diversification will reduce the standard deviation of the portfolio and underlying funds
- The same is generally true of kurtosis
- However, this is not as straight forward for skewness

12.2 Demonstrate knowledge of mean, variance, skewness, and kurtosis of the returns of hedge fund strategies.

For example:

Interpret the statistical moments of return distributions of hedge fund strategies

- The normal distribution is characterized by its first two moments: mean and variance
- Modeling asset returns using normal distribution should be viewed as an approximation as there is some possibility of losses exceeding -100% with a normal distribution
- Hedge fund returns may be nonnormal due to underlying securities with nonnormal returns distributions
  - o Negative skew means that returns well below the mean are observed with much higher frequency than in a normal distribution
  - o Also, the mean is less than its median

12.3 Demonstrate knowledge of various hedge fund strategies.

For example:

Identify the four main types of hedge fund strategies (i.e., directional, event risk, absolute return, and diversified) and their characteristics

- Directional
  - o e.g., equity hedge and short bias funds
  - o Usually retain some market exposure
- Event driven – put option exposure
  - o Event driven and relative value strategies historically have the lowest standard deviation but the largest values of negative skewness and excess kurtosis; strategies consistently earn small profits but are prone to posting large losses over short periods of time
  - o Event risk is basically an off-balance-sheet-risk since the risk exposure is not explicitly reflected in the financials (short positions are harder to detect)
- Absolute return
  - o Are often concentrated portfolios that are index agnostic

- Diversified
  - Global macro and systematic diversified funds offered positive skewness of historical returns

Identify and explain the parameters that may be used in a hedge fund investment program

- Parameters will determine how the hedge fund program is constructed and operated
- Should include risk and return targets as well as the type of strategies that may be used
- Should operate at two levels: for the individual hedge fund manager and the overall fund

Recognize the value of parameterization

- Parameters for the individual funds may be different than for the overall program

12.4 Demonstrate knowledge of reasons for incorporating hedge funds into an investment program.

For example:

Recognize the return enhancement and diversification potential of hedge funds as additions to portfolios of traditional assets

- Most hedge fund strategies offer similar or high mean returns of stocks & bonds with lower standard deviation than stocks
- Risk management benefit as well

Describe and recognize the characteristics and potential benefits of opportunistic hedge fund investing

- Major goal is to seek attractive returns through locating superior underlying investments
- Can be used to expand the set of available investments
- Ability to add alpha by shorting investments

List the empirical evidence regarding the results of adding hedge funds to portfolios of traditional assets

- Diversification benefits (correlation significantly less than 1)
- Consistent positive performance

12.5 Demonstrate knowledge of research regarding the relationship between hedge funds trading and market volatility.

For example:

Discuss the conclusions of empirical studies regarding the relationship between trading by hedge fund managers and the level of market volatility

- Results of Khandani and Lo
  - Hedge fund industry has facilitated economic growth and generated social benefits (providing liquidity, engaging in price discovery, discerning new sources of returns, facilitating the transfer of risk)

- Hedge funds that engage in short selling may actually reduce market volatility as they seek to sell assets as prices rise and buy assets as prices fall

12.6 Demonstrate knowledge of hedge fund indices.

For example:

Describe the challenges of accounting for the effects of management and incentive fees in hedge fund indices

- Subtracting forecasted incentive fees from monthly performance numbers may lead to estimation errors since the forecasted fees may be different from actual fees collected at year end
- Negotiated investment terms will vary across funds
- The more successful a hedge fund manager is, the more likely it is that he will increase his fees (fee bias)

Compare asset-weighted hedge fund indices and equal-weighted hedge fund indices

- Asset-weighted
  - The largest funds are the most represented in an index
  - More accurately reflects the market impact experienced by the majority of the money invested in hedge funds
  - Many other assets are benchmarked against other market-cap weighted indices
- Equal-weighted
  - Returns from each fund are equally represented in the index
  - Advantage of not favoring strategies that attract a lot of capital (e.g., global macro, relative value)

Recognize the concepts of representativeness and data biases (e.g., survivorship, selection, instant history, liquidation) and their effects on hedge fund returns reported by databases

- Survivorship bias
  - Can be measured as the average return of surviving funds in excess of the average return of all funds
  - Estimated at 2.6% to 5% per year
  - Usually affects databases and not indices – historical performance of funds that fail are still included in the historical performance of the index
- Selection bias
  - Hedge fund managers report voluntarily and an index may disproportionately reflect those managers who choose to report
  - However, successful managers may choose not to report after reaching capacity and not needing to raise new funds
- Instant history bias (backfill bias)
  - When a database backfills historical performance of a fund that predates when the manager was added to the database
  - Hedge fund managers are more likely to report after a period of good performance

- Similar to survivorship bias, this bias does not affect the historical performance of an index since most index providers do not revise the historical performance of an index when a new manager is added
- Liquidation – fund managers typically cease reporting before they're shut down

Recognize the challenges involved in defining hedge fund strategies and the effect of style drift

- Hedge fund managers may be classified differently by different index providers
- Often there is a lack of specificity in the hedge fund offering documents with regards to the strategy employed
- Hedge funds are not required to notify an index provider if they adapt their strategy (style drift)
- Trend from single strategy to multistrategy funds

Identify issues that determine investability of hedge fund indices

- Capacity limitations on hedge fund investments
- An index could have closed funds – less investability

Chapter 13: Macro and Managed Futures Funds

Keywords

Black-box trading models: Use of electronic platforms for entering trading orders with an algorithm which executes pre-programmed trading instructions whose variables may include timing, price, or quantity of the order, or in many cases initiating the order without human intervention.

Breakout strategies: Used by active investors to take a position within a trend's early stages.

Capacity: The quantity of capital that a fund can deploy without substantial reduction in risk-adjusted performance.

Capacity risk: Risk that arises when a managed futures trader is concentrating its trades in a market that lacks enough depth (i.e., liquidity).

Commodity pools: Investment structure where many individual investors combine their moneys and trade in futures contracts as a single entity in order to gain leverage.

Commodity trading advisors: Asset managers who focus on trading in the currency or commodity futures markets.

Conditional correlation coefficient: A correlation coefficient calculated on a subset of observations that is selected using a condition.

Counterparty risk: The risk to each party of a contract that the counterparty will not live up to its contractual obligations.

Countertrend strategies: A trading strategy where an investor attempts to make small gains through a series of trades against the current trend.

Degradation: The tendency and process through time by which a trading rule or trading system declines in effectiveness.

Discretionary fund trading: Discretionary trading is carried out by investment managers who identify and select investments; systematic trading is based on mathematical models and executed by software with limited human involvement beyond the programming and updating of the software.

Event risk: The risk due to unforeseen events partaken by or associated with a company

Exponential moving average: A type of moving average that is similar to a simple moving average, except that more weight is given to the latest data. It is a geometrically declining moving average based on a weighted parameter, λ.

Fundamental: Fundamental analysis of a business involves analyzing its financial statements and health, its management and competitive advantages, and its competitors and markets.

Global macro funds: Strategy of investing on a large scale around the world using economic theory to justify the decision making process. The strategy is typically based on forecasts and analysis about interest rates trends, the general flow of funds, political changes, government policies, inter-government relations, and other broad systemic factors.

Individually managed futures account: A managed futures account that is not pooled with other investors.

Leverage risk: Funds that use significant leverage may be forced to deploy additional capital or liquidate positions if they experience losses.

Liquidity risk: Refers to the risk associated with trading in a thinly-traded market that will affect securities prices.

Managed futures: Active trading of futures and forward contracts on physical commodities, financial assets, and exchange rates.

Market risk: Exposure in unexpected changes in market directions.

Mean-reverting: The extent to which an asset's price moves toward the average of its recent price levels.

MLMI (Mount Lucas Management Index): The MLM Index™ is a diversified portfolio of 22 liquid futures contracts traded on U.S. and foreign exchanges. Sectors traded include commodities, currencies and global fixed income.

Model risk: Risk that arises when an algorithmic model is not adequately tested before deployment and therefore could break down under particular market conditions.

Momentum: When a movement in a security price tends to be followed by subsequent movements of the same security in the same direction.

Moving average: Method used to analyze a set of data points by creating a series of averages of different subsets of the full data set.

Natural hedger: A market participant who seeks to hedge risk that springs from its fundamental business activities rather than earn profits via speculation.

Pattern recognition systems: Strategies that attempt to capture non-trend based but predictable abnormal market behavior in prices or volatilities.

Private commodity pools: Investment funds that invest in the futures markets that are sold privately to high net worth investors and institutional investors.

Public commodity pools: Investment funds that invest in the futures markets that are open to the public.

Random walk: The theory that stock price changes have the same distribution and are independent of each other, so the past movement or trend of a stock price or market cannot be used to predict its future movement.

Regulatory risk: The tendency for futures exchanges to be especially prone to a change in margin terms or to face actions by governmental entities that tax or restrict futures trading.

Robustness: Refers to the reliability with which a model or system developed for a particular application or data set can be successfully extended into other applications and/or data sets.

Simple moving average: A simple, or arithmetic, moving average that is calculated by adding the closing price of the security for a number of time periods and then dividing this total by the number of time periods. Short-term averages respond quickly to changes in the price of the underlying, while long-term averages are slow to react.

Slippage: With regard to futures contracts as well as other financial instruments, slippage is the difference between estimated transaction costs and the amount actually paid. Brokers may not always be effective enough at executing orders. Market-impacted, liquidity, and frictional costs may also contribute. Algorithmic trading is often used to reduce slippage.

Systematic fund trading: Systematic trading is based on mathematical models and executed by software with limited human involvement beyond the programming and updating of the software.

Technical analysis: Analysis of an investment using price and volume data.

Transparency risk: Lack of detailed information regarding an investment portfolio or strategy.

Trend-following strategies: Strategies designed to take advantage of momentum in price momentum.

Validation: Refers to the use of new data or new methodologies to test a trading rule developed on another set of data or with another methodology.

Weighted moving average: A weighted average is any average that has multiplying factors to give different weights to data at different positions in the sample window. Usually formed as an arithmetically declining average of more distant prices.

Whipsawing: When a trader alternates between establishing long positions immediately before price declines and short positions immediately before price increases, resulting in a series of losses.

Learning Objectives

13.1 Demonstrate knowledge of major distinctions within the category of macro and managed futures funds.

For example:

Distinguish between discretionary fund trading and systematic fund trading

- Discretionary fund trading: trading decisions made by people
- Systematic fund trading: trading decisions made by computers

Define technical analysis and fundamental analysis and discuss the reasons for pursuing each

- Technical analysis
  - Based on the idea that prices already incorporate some economic information but price patterns may be identified that could be exploited for profit opportunities
  - Prices may not instantaneously and completely reflect all available information
  - There is also a belief that market prices are determined by trading activity unrelated to a rational analysis of underlying economic information
- Fundamental analysis – uses underlying financial and economic information to determine intrinsic values

13.2 Demonstrate knowledge of global macro funds.

For example:

Describe the key characteristics of global macro funds

- Whereas macro funds are concentrated in specific markets or themes, global macro funds exercise their strategy on a global basis
- Can invest widely across currencies, commodities, financial markets, geographies

Recognize the main risks (i.e., market, event, and leverage) of macro investing

- Market risk: Macro funds don't usually focus on equity markets as equities can be highly influenced by microeconomic factors (company-specific events). But macro funds can take concentrated risks in currency, commodity and sovereign debt markets.
- Event risk: Macro funds attempt to profit from event risk and large market dislocations especially involving government financial policies.
- Leverage: May be forced to liquidate positions if they are unable to deploy additional capital after a period of losses.

13.3 Demonstrate knowledge of the historical performance of macro investing.

For example:

Recognize inferences that can be drawn from comparing definable characteristics of macro investing with its historical stand-alone and portfolio performance

- High return and low risk relative to equities and bonds
- Relatively unscathed by 2007 financial crisis (provided downside protection)
- Moderate diversification benefits

13.4 Demonstrate knowledge of managed futures.

For example:

Describe the key characteristics of managed futures funds

- Goal is to enhance returns rather than for diversification benefits
- Tend to be based more on systematic trading (rather than discretionary)
- Managers tend to use more technical analysis

Discuss regulation, background, and organizational structures (i.e., public commodity pools, private commodity pools, and individually managed accounts) of the managed futures industry

- Regulation & Background
    - Were largely unregulated until the early 1970s
    - 1974 in US – Commodity Exchange Act (CEA) and CFTC created
    - Congress established standards for financial reporting, offering memorandum disclosure and bookkeeping
- Organizational structures
    - Public commodity pools – Low minimum investment and high liquidity for investors
    - Private commodity pools – Lower fees and greater flexibility to implement investment strategies
    - Individually managed accounts – Investor retains custody of the assets, maintains transparency and control and can increase or decrease leverage applied

13.5 Demonstrate knowledge of systematic trading.

For example:

Identify methods for and issues involved in deriving systematic trading rules

- Systematic trading rules are generally derived using backtests of the individual trading strategies

Recognize key questions to ask when evaluating individual trading strategies

- What is the trading system and how was it developed?
- Why does the trading system work and why might it not work?
- How is the trading system implemented?

Describe key components of methods used to validate systematic trading rules and the detection and effects of trading rule degradation

- Validation of the trading rule should be performed with data that were not directly used to develop that trading rule
- It is vital to know how many trading rules were tested, subject to validation and rejected; with a confidence interval of 95%, 5% will automatically survive a validation process unless the validation process is carefully designed to incorporate into its statistical approach the total number of tests performed

13.6 Demonstrate knowledge of systematic trading strategies.

For example:

Describe the characteristics of trend-following strategies

- Uses recent price movements over some time period to identify a price trend
- The goal is to establish long positions in assets experiencing upward trends and establish short positions in assets experiencing downward trends

Define and apply simple moving averages, weighted moving averages, and exponential moving averages

- See Keywords

Define and apply breakout trading rules

- Focuses on identifying the beginning of a new trend by observing the range of recent market prices
- If the current market price is below all prices in the range, this is a breakout and possibly the beginning of a downward trend → initiate short position
- If the current market price is above all prices in the range, this is a breakout and possibly the beginning of an upward trend → initiate long position

List the conclusions of research on the nature and efficacy of trend-following strategies

- Dominant strategy applied in managed futures
- Two drawbacks (Lhabitant)
  - They are slow to recognize the start or end of trends
  - Moving average rules are designed to exploit trends or momentum that should not persist in competitive markets; perfect competition causes randomness rather than trending in price
- Sometimes described as long volatility strategies

Describe the characteristics of non-trend-following strategies

- Designed to profit from nonrandomness in market movements
- Countertrend strategies – Use various statistical measures (e.g., price oscillation, relative strength index) to identify range-trading opportunities
- Pattern recognition

Describe the characteristics of relative value strategies

- Attempts to exploit inefficient short-term price divergences between two correlated prices or rates
- In managed futures, this strategy analyzes the correlation structure between two or more futures contracts and attempts to exploit deviation in prices as individual contracts respond differently to new information or to liquidity imbalances

13.7 Demonstrate knowledge of empirical research on managed futures.

For example:

Discuss empirical evidence regarding the downside risk protection offered by managed futures

- The conditional correlation coefficient indicates that they do not experience the strong correlation to stocks in down markets
- Managed futures had zero to positive correlation to stocks in up markets and negative correlation in down markets
- Macro and managed futures funds were close to normally distributed with skewness near zero

Describe the reasons why managed futures might provide superior returns

- CTAs are more likely to earn positive alphas in those markets in which there is a great need for hedging when natural hedgers come to market at different points in time

Describe the risks of managed futures funds

- Transparency risk of black boxes
- Model risk if they are inadequately tested
- Capacity risk if trades are concentrated in a market without enough depth
- Liquidity risk if a thinly-traded market. Can also arise in a high volume market trading volume among other market participants declines and managed futures funds become a larger proportion of the trading volume

13.9 Demonstrate knowledge of historical performance of managed futures and macro funds.

For example:

Recognize inferences that can be drawn from comparing definable characteristics of managed futures and macro investing with their historical stand-alone and portfolio performance

- Higher returns and volatility
- Diversification benefits due to modest correlations with stocks and bonds
- Downside protection

Chapter 14: Event-Driven Hedge Funds

Keywords

Activist investment strategy: An activist shareholder uses an equity stake in a corporation to put public pressure on its management. The goals of activist shareholders range from financial (increase of shareholder value through changes in corporate policy, financing structure, cost cutting, etc.) to non-financial (disinvestment from particular countries, adoption of environmentally friendly policies, etc.).

Agency costs: The cost to a "principal" (an organization, person or group of persons), when the principal chooses or hires an "agent" to act on its behalf. Because the two parties have different interests and the agent has more information, the principal cannot directly ensure that its agent is always acting in its (the principals') best interests

Agency theory: Concerns the difficulties in motivating one party (the "agent"), to act in the best interests of another (the "principal") rather than in his or her own interests.

Bankruptcy process: Allocates firm assets across various security holders and stakeholders when the value of the firm's liabilities exceed the value of its assets.

Bidding contest: When two or more firms compete to acquire the same target.

Capital structure arbitrage: Investment strategy that seeks to take advantage of disparities between different equities and debt products issued by the same company. Investors using the strategy will spot such a disparity and then buy or sell assets based on the logical assumption that the market will correct the disparity. Unlike some other forms of arbitrage, capital structure arbitrage does not purport to offer a guaranteed profit.

Compensation scheme: Agreement specifying payments to an agent for services rendered.

Corporate governance: Describes the processes and people that control the decisions of a corporation.

Distressed debt hedge funds: Hedge funds that invest in distressed securities (securities of companies or government entities that are either already in default, under bankruptcy protection, or in distress and heading toward such a condition).

Event-driven: Hedge fund investment strategy that seeks to exploit pricing inefficiencies that may occur before or after a corporate event, such as an earnings call, bankruptcy, merger, acquisition, or spinoff.

Event driven multi-strategy funds: Funds that diversify across a wide variety of event-driven strategies.

Event risk: The risk due to unforeseen events partaken by or associated with a company

Financial market segmentation: When two or more markets use different valuations for similar assets due to the lack of participants who trade in both markets or who perform arbitrage between the markets.

Financing risk: The ability of the acquiring firm to raise the cash necessary to acquire the target firm in a merger proposal.

Freerider: A person or entity who allows others to pay initial costs and then benefits from those expenditures.

Interlocking boards: Refers to the practice of members of a corporate board of directors serving on the boards of multiple corporations.

Liquidation process: When all of the firm's assets are sold and the cash proceeds are distributed to creditors.

Long binary call option: A way of looking at event strategy returns using call options. The hedge fund is long in the merger target and the position can be viewed as a long position in a riskless bond with a face value of the lower price of the stock if the deal fails and a long position in a binary call option that pays if the deal is consummated and is worthless if the deal fails.

Long binary put option: A way of looking at event strategy returns using put options. A hedge fund's long position in a merger target can be viewed as a long position in a riskless bond with a face value equal to the price of the merger target if the deal succeeds and a short position in a binary put option that pays the reduction in the share price of the merger target if the deal fails.

Merger arbitrage: A hedge fund strategy in which the stocks of two merging companies are simultaneously bought and sold to create a profit.

Naked option position: When the investors is short an option position but does not have a hedged position (owning the underlying asset in the case of writing a call, being short the underlying asset when writing a put).

One-off transaction: A transaction so unique that it requires specialized skill, knowledge and/or effort to execute. Describes most distressed transactions.

Principal-agent relationship: A relationship in which the principal hires an agent to perform decision-making tasks.

Proxy battle: Fight between the firm's current management and shareholder activists to obtain proxies from shareholders.

Recovery rate: Portion of the face value of a bond that is ultimately received by an investor at the end of the bankruptcy proceedings.

Recovery value: The value of each security in the firm.

Reorganization process: The process that aims to stabilize the operations and finances of the company that allows it to continue operations after the bankruptcy process has been completed.

Selling insurance: When event driven hedge funds earn relatively small returns for providing relatively large protection against risks.

Shareholder activism: Efforts by shareholders to influence the decisions of a firm in a direction contrary to firm management.

Special situation funds: Funds with a focus on special situations, which are particular circumstances involving a security that would compel investors to trade the security based on the special situation, rather than the underlying fundamentals of the security or some other investment rationale. An investment made due to a special situation is typically an attempt to profit from a change in valuation as a result of the special situation, and is generally not a long-term investment.

Stock-for-stock merger proposals: When an acquirer offers to purchase the target company using shares of its stock (stock-for-stock swap).

Traditional merger arbitrage: Strategy that uses leverage to buy the stock of the target firm and sells short the stock of the acquiring firm.

Learning Objectives

14.1 Demonstrate knowledge of the sources of event-driven strategy returns.

For example:

Explain the insurance-selling view of event-driven strategy returns

- Earning relatively small returns for providing relatively large protection against risks

Explain the binary option view of event-driven strategy returns

- An event-driven strategy can be thought of as a long binary call option or long binary put option

14.2 Demonstrate knowledge of activist investing.

For example:

Define activist investing and identify the components of activist investment strategies

Strategy involves the following:

- Identifying corporations with management that is not maximizing shareholder wealth
- The establishment of investment positions that can benefit from particular changes in corporate governance such as the replacement of the existing management
- The execution of the corporate governance changes that are perceived to benefit established investment positions

Recognize the structure of corporate governance

- Board of Directors selects the executive management team
- Management runs the company day-to-day
- Agency conflicts exist

Identify types of shareholder activists and the key players in financial activism

- Financial vs. social activists
- Activists vs. pacifists
- Initiators vs. followers
- Friendly vs. hostile activists
- Active vs. passive activists

Discuss agency costs and the conflicts of interest between shareholders and managers

- Explains why executive management does not act to unlock the intrinsic value of a company without pressure from activists
- Not all conflicts of interests can be cost-effectively resolved and it is sometimes cheaper for shareholders to accept managerial actions that conflict with the shareholders' best interests rather than try to perfectly align manager and shareholder interests

Recognize and discuss approaches commonly used by activist investors to generate alpha

- Seeking to expedite change to company operations
- The activist usually publicizes an issue that is believed to add substantial value to the shares of a target firm

Recognize inferences that can be drawn from comparing definable characteristics of activist investing with its historical stand-alone and portfolio performance

- Consistently positive correlation to global equities, commodities, changes in credit spreads and changes in equity volatility
- Insignificant correlation to global bonds and US high yield bonds

14.3 Demonstrate knowledge of merger arbitrage.

For example:

Recognize the characteristics of traditional merger arbitrage

- Use leverage to buy stock of target
- Short sell stock of acquirer
- Strategy cannot be used for small firms with insufficient liquidity to short positions

Recognize the characteristics of stock-for-stock mergers

- Acquirer purchases target using its stock
- Speculators take offsetting hedged positions in the shares of the two firms based on the ratio of shares in the merger offer
- Long positions in the target stock are exposed to event risk between the time of merger announcement and completion (or failure)

Discuss the effects of third-party bidders and bidding wars on merger arbitrage

- Traditional merger arbitrage benefits from a bidding war which can create large returns but are the riskiest situations
- Merger arbitrage funds tend to make money slowly (over 6-18 months as the target price approaches the deal price) and lose money quickly
- Results in negative skewness and excess kurtosis of returns

Describe regulatory risk in the context of merger arbitrage

- Various US and foreign regulatory agencies may not allow a proposed merger to take place
- The concern is typically that the merger could reduce competition in a given market
- Other reasons can be nationalistic or tax-related
- Commodity-producing firms or firms tied to national defense are especially politically sensitive

Describe financing risk in the context of merger arbitrage

- The acquiring firm may not be able to raise the necessary funds to purchase the target
- For stock swap deals, investors focus on regulatory issues and the fit between the two firms
- Financing risk arises when there is a cash component to the deal
- LBO's are particularly sensitive to financing risk

Recognize inferences that can be drawn from comparing definable characteristics of merger arbitrage with its historical stand-alone and portfolio performance

- Low volatility and high Sharpe ratio
- No correlation to global bonds
- Diversification benefits

14.4 Demonstrate knowledge of distressed securities hedge funds.

For example:

Distinguish between distressed debt strategies in hedge funds and in private equity

- Private equity investors take a long-term view on the value and reorganization potential of the corporation
- Hedge funds typically take a short-term trading view

Identify key components of the bankruptcy process

- In the US, firms declaring bankruptcy may liquidate or reorganize operations
- In Europe, firms typically face liquidation if they are unable to meet debt obligations

Define a naked option position

- Shares in highly leveraged firms resemble call options
- Short-selling distressed securities is comparable to writing naked call options on the firm's assets
- Generates a negatively skewed return distribution

Describe the risks and returns of short sales of distressed equities

- Shares can rally before exiting bankruptcy especially if assets are worth more than debt

Describe considerations involved in buying undervalued securities and estimating the recovery value of distressed securities

- The recovery value of distressed securities at liquidation can be especially sensitive to industry market conditions
- The time that firms can spend in bankruptcy can vary widely

Recognize activist approaches to investing in distressed securities

- Activist investors in distressed securities seek to influence both the recovery value and the timing of the exit from the bankruptcy process

Describe the characteristics of capital structure arbitrage

- Strategy has a reduced exposure to the general risks of the company and are plays within the firm's capital structure
- A traditional capital structure arbitrage trade involves buying a more senior claim and selling short the more junior claim
- The key to profitability is when the more senior security improves more (or deteriorates less) than the junior security

Explain the strategy of buying distressed firms using distressed securities

- Can buy with an intention of gaining a controlling interest or buy the securities of a distressed company shortly before it announces its reorganization plan to the bankruptcy court

Recognize inferences that can be drawn from comparing definable characteristics of distressed securities funds with their historical stand-alone and portfolio performance

- Strong returns, relatively low volatility, strong Sharpe ratio
- Negatively skewed returns and leptokurtic
- Relatively unscathed by some global events but experienced large losses in the 2007 financial crisis
- Limited diversification benefits with distressed strategies involving equities; greater diversification benefits with distressed strategies involving bonds

14.5 Demonstrate knowledge of event-driven multi-strategy funds.

For example:

Describe key characteristics of event-driven multi-strategy funds

- Diversify across a number of event-driven strategies
- Because merger activity and debt defaults are countercyclical, combining the two strategies can increase fund capacity and smooth returns

Chapter 15: Relative Value Hedge Funds

Keywords

Anticipated volatility: The future level of volatility expected by a market participant.

Asset-backed securities: A financial security backed by a loan, lease or receivables against assets other than real estate and mortgage-backed securities.

Busted convertibles: A convertible security that is trading well below its conversion value. The result is that the security is valued as regular debt because there is very little chance that it will ever reach the convertible price before maturity.

Carry trades: The FX carry trade seeks to profit from the failure of uncovered interest rate parity to work in the short run. In an FX carry trade, the investor invests in a high-yield currency while borrowing in a low-yield currency. If the higher yield currency does not depreciate by the interest rate differential, the investor makes a profit.

Classic convertible bond arbitrage trade: Trade that involves the purchase of an undervalued convertible bond and a short position in the underlying equity.

Classic dispersion trade: A market-neutral, short correlation trade that is popular among volatility arbitrage practitioners. It typically takes a long position in options listed on equities of *single* companies (creating a basket of options on individual securities that mimics the index) and short positions in a related *index* option.

Classic relative value strategy trade: Trade that involves taking a long position in an underpriced security and a short position in an overpriced security.

Complexity premium: A higher expected return of a security to compensate the investor for analyzing and managing a position that requires additional time and expertise. Also predicts that a complex security's price is higher (and thus the rate of return is lower) than that of a simple security with identical payoff distribution. The intuition is that fund managers are willing to pay a "complexity premium" because a complex security potentially allows them to influence investor beliefs and attract additional fees.

Components of convertible arbitrage returns: The income component (coupon interest received from the bond, dividends paid on the short stock position, and rebates earned on the short stock position), plus the capital gains from the stock and bond.

Convergence: The return of prices or rates to relative values that are deemed normal.

Convertible bonds: The owner of a convertible bond can exchange the bond for the common shares of the issuer. A convertible bond includes an embedded call option giving the bondholder the right to buy the common stock of the issuer. Almost all convertible bonds are callable, and some convertible issues are putable.

Correlation risk: Risk due to changes in realized or anticipated levels of correlation between market prices or rates.

Correlations go to one: During periods of financial turbulence, stocks and bonds move down in value together.

Counterparty risk: The risk to each party of a contract that the counterparty will not live up to its contractual obligations.

Delta: Measures change in the option price per one dollar change in the underlying stock's price; alternatively, the change in the option price equals the change in the underlying multiplied by the option's delta.

Delta-neutral: The goal of a delta-neutral portfolio (or delta-neutral hedge) is to combine a long position in a stock with a short position in a call option so that the portfolio value does not change when the stock value changes. In addition, the value-weighted sum of all deltas of all positions equals zero.

Duration: Weighted average of the times until those fixed cash flows are received. When an asset is considered as a function of yield, duration also measures the price sensitivity to yield, the rate of change of price with respect to yield or the percentage change in price for a parallel shift in yields.

Duration-neutral: A duration neutral portfolio can be thought of as exhibiting zero deviation in price over all interest rate paths. It's also a portfolio in which the aggregated durations of the short positions equal the aggregated durations of the long position weighted by value.

Effective duration: Assumes that yield changes may change expected cash flows. For embedded options, a change in yield may alter cash flows and hence this measure of Duration is more appropriate.

Equity-like convertible: The further in the money that the option is, the more the convertible bond behaves like the underlying stock.

Fixed-income arbitrage: Involves simultaneous long and short positions in fixed-income securities with the expectation that the securities prices will converge.

Gamma: The sensitivity of delta to the change in a price of the underlying asset. The second derivative of an option's price with respect to the price of the underlying asset or the first derivative of delta with respect to the price of the underlying asset.

General collateral stocks: Stocks not facing heavy borrowing demand.

Hybrid convertibles: Convertible bonds with moderately sized conversion ratios and stock options closer to being at the money. Hybrids are typically the most attractive bonds for use in convertible arbitrage strategies due to their asymmetric payoff profile.

Implied volatility: The standard deviation of returns that is viewed as being consistent with an observed market price. It is also the volatility that, when used in the Black-Scholes formula, produces the current market price of the option. Implied volatility can be estimated using observed prices for interest rate derivatives and option pricing models.

Intercurve arbitrage positions: Arbitrage using different yield curves (e.g., swap spread trading – arbitraging the difference in swap rates – and carry trades).

Interest rate immunization: Strategy that ensures that a change in interest rates will not affect the value of a portfolio.

Intracurve arbitrage positions: Arbitrage using the same yield curve.

Marking-to-market: Also known as fair value accounting this practice refers to accounting for the "fair value" of an asset or liability based on the current market price. Mark-to-market accounting can change values on the balance sheet as market conditions change. In contrast, historical cost accounting, based on the past transactions, is simpler, more stable, and easier to perform, but does not represent current market value.

Marking-to-model: The practice of pricing a position or portfolio at prices determined by financial models, in contrast to allowing the market to determine the price.

Modified duration: Duration calculation that assumes that yield changes do not change expected cash flows. This assumption makes sense for option-free bonds.

Moneyness: The extent to which an option is in the money, at the money, or out the money.

Mortgage-backed securities arbitrage: Attempts to generate low risk profits through the relative mispricing between MBS or between MBS and other fixed income securities.

Option-adjusted spread: The flat spread which has to be added to the treasury yield curve in a pricing model (that accounts for embedded options) to discount a security payment to match its market price.

Parallel shift: Phenomenon that occurs when the interest rate on all maturities increases or decreases by the same number of basis points.

Portfolio insurance: Any financial method used to limit losses from large adverse price movements.

Price transparency: The information on prices and quantities at which market participants are offering to buy and sell an instrument.

Pricing risk: The risk of actual or potential mispricing of positions.

Realized volatility: The actual observed volatility experienced by an asset.

Rebate: A payment of interest to the security's borrower on the collateral posted.

Relative value strategies: Strategies that aim to generate alpha by predicting changes in relationships between prices or rates typically via simultaneous long and short positions that are relatively equal in size, volatility and other risk exposures.

Riding the yield curve: The process of holding a bond as its yield moves up or down through time.

Rolling down: The process of experiencing decreasing yields to maturity as an asset's maturity declines through time in an upward sloping yield curve environment.

Short correlation: A trade that generates profits from low levels of realized correlation and losses from high levels of realized correlation (e.g., classic dispersion trade).

Short squeeze: When short sellers are forced to buy shares at increasing prices to cover their positions due to limited liquidity.

Sovereign debt: Bonds issued by a national government in a foreign currency, in order to finance the issuing country's growth.

Special stock: A stock that demands higher net fees when it is borrowed (as in a short sale). To a short seller, this means receiving a smaller rebate.

Tail risk: The risk of an asset or portfolio of assets moving more than 3 standard deviations from its current price.

Term structure of interest rates: The relationship between interest rates or bond yields and different terms or maturities.

Theta: Measures the sensitivity of the value of the derivative to the passage of time - the "time decay." Can be measured as the first derivative of an option price with respect to time to expiration of the option. Theta is negative for a long position in an option.

Variance notional value: Scales the size of the cash flows in a variance swap to the dollar value per variance unit.

Variance swaps: Commonly traded by volatility arbitrage funds, variance swaps are forward contracts whereby one party agree to make a cash payment to the other party based on the realized variance of a price or rate in exchange for receiving a predetermined cash flow.

Vega: Measures option price sensitivity to volatility.

Vega notional value: Scales the contract to the dollar value per Vega or volatility point.

Vega risk: Risk associated with changes in the volatility of a price, return or rate.

Volatility risk: Risk due to changes in realized or anticipated levels of volatility in a market price or rate.

Volatility swap: Mirrors the variance swap except that the payoff of the contract is based on the standard deviation of returns instead of the variance.

Yield curve: Curve showing several yields or interest rates across different contract lengths (2 month, 2 year, 20 year, etc...) for a similar debt contract.

Learning Objectives

15.1 Demonstrate knowledge of relative value hedge funds.

For example:

Define and describe relative value strategies

- Rather than trying to predict the price of a security, relative value strategies attempt to profit from converging prices

Define and describe the classic relative value strategy trade

- Involves taking a long position in the underpriced security and a short position in the overpriced security

Define and describe the classic convertible arbitrage trade

- Purchase an undervalued convertible bond and hedge the risk with a short position on the underlying equity

Define convertible bonds and apply the unbundling approach for pricing convertible bonds

- Valuing convertible bonds is typically done by unbundling it into its component parts of straight debt and the equity call option (Black-Scholes) and summing their values

Define busted, hybrid, and equity-like convertibles

- See Keywords

Define and describe the concepts of delta, gamma, and theta

- See Keywords

Explain the effects of gamma and volatility on the profitability of a delta neutral position

- Positive gamma of the convertible bond generates profit
- A delta hedge with a low gamma will work better for a given change in the asset price as a result
- Gamma is greater the less the time to expiration and the closer the exercise price is to the asset price
- Out-of-the-money options and longer-term options have lower gammas and thus are better for constructing a dynamic hedge (the hedge has less gamma risk)

Discuss short selling in the context of convertible arbitrage

- The most common convertible arbitrage strategy involves short selling large quantities of the underlying common stock

Recognize the role complexity plays in making convertible bond arbitrage attractive to some hedge fund managers

- As a small and complex asset class, convertible bonds may offer liquidity and/or complexity premiums to skilled hedge fund managers employing the strategy

Identify the four reasons that issuers may continue to offer convertible bonds at attractive prices

- Issuers may underestimate the true costs of their issuance and not fully appreciate the potential harm to share prices from dilution
- Because they are sold as 144A securities and can only be sold to institutions, their prices are lower and returns higher as a premium for bearing liquidity risk
- Convertible bonds reduce agency costs since any increase in volatility benefits convertible bondholders as well as equity holders and their prices are less sensitive to the credit risk of the issuing firm
- The signal conveyed to the market of issuing convertible bonds is not as negative as when equity is issued (think 'pecking order theory')

Identify the components of convertible arbitrage returns

Convertible bond arbitrage income	+	Convertible bond and stock net capital gains/losses
Bond interest received – Stock dividends paid on short stock position + Short stock rebate on cash proceeds – Financing expenses on leveraged position	+	Capital gains on stock and bond - Capital losses on stock and bond

Recognize and discuss return drivers and risks of convertible bond arbitrage

Return drivers

- Minor differences in the volatility assumptions used to price the embedded stock option can generate significant price differences
- Leverage

Risks

- Interest rates
- Equity and volatility
- Correlation – the strategy is long correlation. As interest rates rise, losses may be offset by gains on the short equity positions. When correlation declines, stock and bond prices move in opposite directions causing losses on both components of the convertible bond
- Credit risk – as credit spreads widen, bond prices fall
- Legal/regulatory
- Liquidity and crisis: Convertible bond investors sell economic disaster insurance, as credit spreads widen during times of economic crisis

Recognize inferences that can be drawn from comparing definable characteristics of convertible arbitrage funds with their historical stand-alone and portfolio performance

- Returns similar to global bonds, high yield bonds, and commodities but with lower volatility

- Strong Sharpe ratio
- Experienced a much greater decline and recovery related to the 2007 financial crisis
- Negatively skewed with very high kurtosis – much higher than traditional investments

15.2 Demonstrate knowledge of volatility arbitrage.

For example:

Define and describe the concepts of vega and anticipated volatility

- See Keywords

Recognize instruments used by volatility arbitrage funds

- Variance swaps - based on variance
- Volatility swaps – based on standard deviation

Identify and apply the approach for determining the final payoff of a variance swap and a volatility swap

- Variance swap payoff $= \frac{Vega\ notional\ value*(realized\ variance-strike\ variance)}{2*\sqrt{strike\ variance}}$
- Volatility swap payoff = Vega notional * (realized volatility – strike volatility)

Compare the risks of exchange-traded derivatives and over-the-counter (OTC) derivatives

- Exchange-traded derivatives offer less counterparty risk
- Exchange-traded derivatives offer more transparency and less pricing risk
- Exchange-traded derivatives offer higher liquidity

Recognize the types of volatility arbitrage strategies

- Typically take long positions in instruments where volatility is underpriced and short positions where volatility is overpriced
- Other market risks are hedged out leaving the fund with less directional risk to the underlying markets
- The positions are instead exposed to volatility risk and correlation risk
- Two types of volatility arbitrage funds: market neutral and those that are intentionally exposed to volatility (typically long)

Discuss the characteristics of market-neutral volatility funds

- Strategy that assumes that there is an arbitrage opportunity between the higher implied volatility and the lower realized volatility of some options

Recognize the challenges of estimating and forecasting dispersion

- There are many ways to calculate dispersion
- Variance swaps generate payoffs nonlinearly related to volatility

Discuss the characteristics of tail risk strategies and how their performance depends on correlation among assets

- Tail risk strategies provide portfolio protection without the large cost of buying put options that expire worthless
- During periods of market stress, correlations among different assets can go to one (move down in price together)

Discuss the characteristics of dispersion trades

- The classic dispersion trade typically takes a long position in options listed on the equities of single companies and short positions in a related index option
- Popular among volatility arbitrage traders
- The relationship between a portfolio of options and a single option on a portfolio is driven by volatility
- Profits are high when the realized correlation is higher than the implied correlation
- Profits are greatest during times of declining correlation and loses when correlations rise significantly

Recognize inferences that can be drawn from comparing definable characteristics of volatility arbitrage funds with their historical stand-alone and portfolio performance

- Low returns but modest volatility and Sharpe ratio
- Negative skew and modest leptokurtosis
- No correlation or beta with other indices except for changes in the VIX

15.3 Demonstrate knowledge of fixed-income arbitrage.

For example:

Discuss duration-neutrality, leverage, and liquidity in the context of fixed income arbitrage

- Duration-neutrality
  - When returns are insensitive to changes in interest rates
  - Most fixed income arbitrage trades are constructed this way
- Leverage: Strategy typically has just small potential profits. Fund managers can use leverage to enhance return
- Liquidity: If positions are maintained or increased as losses mount, the fund may be forced to liquidate when price discrepancies are at their highest levels

Recognize types and characteristics of fixed-income arbitrage strategies

- Sovereign debt
  - Riding the yield curve
  - Rolling down
- Corporate debt
- Asset-backed or MBS

Discuss the risks and returns of sovereign debt in fixed-income arbitrage strategies

- Governments can choose to default even if they are technically able to meet obligations
- Most governments can use monetary policy to alter the value of their currency and change the value of their obligations

Recognize the characteristics of asset-backed and mortgage-backed securities strategies& arbitrage

- The complexity of valuing ABS makes them a strong candidate for arbitrage
- Risks are also driven by changes in the shape of the yield curve, borrower prepayment and default rates
- Hedging these risks may involve the purchase or sale of MBS products or other derivative products
- The use of OTC for hedging adds counterparty risk

Discuss the effects of prepayment risk and option-adjusted spreads on asset-backed and mortgage-backed securities strategies

- Hedge funds can use the OAS to evaluate the market prices of ABS
- Prepayment can be linked to interest rates or idiosyncratic factors (e.g., borrower moves) that make it difficult to model

Recognize inferences that can be drawn from comparing definable characteristics of fixed-income arbitrage with its historical stand-alone and portfolio performance

- Moderate returns, volatility and Sharpe ratio
- Large negative skew and kurtosis

15.4 Demonstrate knowledge of relative value multi-strategy funds.

For example:

Describe key characteristics of relative value multi-strategy funds

- Single portfolio that employs a variety of relative value strategies
- Cost-effective diversification

Chapter 16: Equity Hedge Funds

Keywords

130/30 funds: A 130–30 fund is considered a long-short equity fund, meaning it goes both long and short at the same time. The "130" portion stands for 130% exposure to its long portfolio and the "30" portion stands for 30% exposure to its short portfolio.

Accounting accruals: The recognition of value based on anticipation of a transaction.

Asynchronous trading: An example of market inefficiency where news affects more than one stock may be assimilated into the price of stocks with different speeds.

Breadth (of a strategy): The number of independent (the statistical lack of correlation between the bets) active (short-term) bets placed into an active portfolio.

Complexity premium: A higher than expected return offered through consistently lower prices of securities that are difficult to value or analyze and must be priced to offer an incentive to perform the needed analysis and potentially invest.

Earnings momentum: The tendency of earnings changes to be positive correlated.

Earnings surprise: Describes the unexpectedness of an earnings announcement.

Equity long/short funds: Hedge fund strategy that involves buying long equities that are expected to increase in value and selling short equities that are expected to decrease in value.

Equity market-neutral funds: Hedge fund strategy that seeks to exploit investment opportunities unique to some specific group of stocks while maintaining a neutral exposure to broad groups of stocks defined, for example, by sector, industry, market capitalization, country, or region. The strategy holds long/short equity positions, with long positions hedged with short positions in the same and related sectors, so that the equity-market-neutral investor should be little affected by sector-wide events. These funds are relatively insensitive to changes in the underlying stock index.

Fundamental law of active management (FLOAM): Law that identifies two key components of actively managed investment strategies: breadth and skill. It connects breadth and skill to the information ratio:

Information Ratio = Information coefficient $* \sqrt{Breadth}$

Illegal insider trading: Corporate insiders in possession of nonpublic information that could affect an investment's value must not act or induce someone else to act on the information.

Information coefficient: Measures managerial skill as the correlation between managerial return predictions and realized returns.

Informationally efficient: A market where securities reflect available information.

Issuance of new stock: A firm's creation of new shares of common stock.

Legal insider trading: Legal trades by insiders are common, as employees of publicly traded corporations often have stock or stock options. It is perfectly legal for insiders to buy and sell stock in their company as long as the insider is trading on information that is generally available to the public no laws are broken.

Limits to arbitrage: The potential inability or unwillingness of speculators such as hedge fund managers to hold their positions without time constraints or increase their positions without size constraints.

Liquidity: The extent to which transactions can be executed with minimal disruption to prices.

Market anomalies: Investment strategies that are violations of informational market efficiency.

Market impact: The degree of the short-term effects on trades on the sizes and levels of bid prices and offer prices.

Market maker: Market participant that deals securities by selling at the ask price and buying at the bid price, thereby receiving the bid-ask spread as compensation for providing the market with liquidity. Market makers sell to and buy from market takers.

Mean neutrality: When a fund is shown to have zero beta exposure or correlation to the underlying market index.

Model misspecification: A model that omits explanatory variables or incorrectly describes the relationships between variables.

Multiple-factor scoring models: Models that combine the factor scores of a number of independent anomaly signals into a single trading signal.

Net stock issuance: The issuance of new stock minus share repurchases.

Nonactive bets: Positions held to reduce tracing error rather than to serve as return-enhancing active bets.

Overreacting: Short-term price changes that are too large relative to the value changes that should occur in a market with perfect informational efficiency.

Pairs trading: The strategy of matching a long position (in an undervalued security) with a short position (in an overvalued security) in two stocks of the same sector.

Post-earnings-announcement drift: Where investors can profit from positive surprises by buying immediately after the earnings announcement or selling short immediately after a negative earnings surprise.

Price momentum: Trending in prices such that an upward price movement indicates a higher expected price and a downward price movement indicates a lower expected price.

Providing liquidity: Refers to the placement of limit orders or other actions that increase the number of available shares in the market place. Providers of liquidity trade with the purpose of making short-term trading profits.

Share buyback program: When a company purchases its own shares from investors in the open market or through a tender offer.

Short bias funds: A hedge fund strategy that maintains a net short exposure to the market through a combination of short and long positions.

Short interest: The quantity of stock shares that investors have sold short but not yet covered or closed out.

Speculation: Bearing abnormal risk and abnormal expected returns in anticipation of abnormally high expected returns.

Standardized unexpected earnings (SUE): A measure of earnings surprise.

$$SUE = \frac{EPS - Analyst\ Consensus\ EPS\ Estimate}{Standard\ Deviation\ of\ Earnings'\ Misses}$$

Taking liquidity: Refers to the execution of market orders by a market participant to meet portfolio preferences that cause a decrease in the supply of limit orders. The institution is trading to attain its preferred long-term positions.

Test of joint hypotheses: Describes an empirical test of market efficiency that assumes the validity of a model of the risk-return relationship in order to test whether a given trading strategy earns consistent risk-adjusted profits.

Under-reacting: Short-term price changes that are too small relative to the value changes that should occur in a market with perfect informational efficiency.

Variance neutrality: When fund returns are uncorrelated to changes in market risk.

Learning Objectives

16.0 Demonstrate knowledge of equity hedge funds styles.

For example:

Recognize characteristics of various equity hedge funds styles

The differentiator is net market exposure:

- Long/short and 130/30 funds retain positive systematic risk levels
- Equity market neutral funds are relatively insensitive to changes in the stock market
- Short bias funds are net short

16.1 Demonstrate knowledge of sources of return for equity hedge funds.

For example:

Discuss providing liquidity as a source of return for equity hedge funds

- Some hedge funds provide market liquidity by buying at a discount and selling at a premium
- Hedge funds make liquidity; institutions tend to take liquidity

Discuss providing informational efficiency as a source of return for equity hedge funds

- Profits can be made by exploiting the inefficiencies caused by poorly informed traders or traders making decisions based on a behavioral basis rather than based on evidence
- Asynchronous trading is an example of market inefficiency
- Sources of abnormal profits are overreacting & underreacting

Discuss the process of using factor analysis to enhance returns for equity hedge funds

- Some hedge funds analyze the factors that drive equity returns and then try to use those factors to predict price changes and find ex ante alpha

16.2 Demonstrate knowledge of market anomalies.

For example:

Discuss how market efficiency tests are tests of joint hypotheses

- Because the test assumes the validity of a model of the risk-return relationship in order to test whether a given trading strategy earns consistent risk-adjusted profits
- Thus, any finding of consistent superior returns may be caused by model misspecification

Identify issues involved in predicting persistence of market anomalies

- Is statistical result due to spurious correlation or true underlying correlations?
- Even if the statistical results are reliable, is the anomaly expected to continue?

- How long should the manager continue with the strategy when it begins suffering losses?

Describe and apply accounting accruals as potential predictors of ex ante alpha

- Bradshaw, Richardson and Sloan research found that firms with large accruals tend to have negative future earnings surprises and stock price underperformance

Define price momentum and recognize its potential role in generating ex ante alpha

- Chan, Jegadeesh and Lakonishok research found that price momentum appears to prevail using six-month intervals

Define earnings momentum and recognize its potential role in generating ex ante alpha

- Stock prices tend to drift in the same direction of SUE

Define net stock issuance and recognize its potential role in generating ex ante alpha

- Stocks that issue large amounts of new shares tend to see their stock underperform the market

Define insider trading and recognize its potential role in generating ex ante alpha

- Legal insider trading can signal potentially valuable information

16.3 Demonstrate knowledge of the fundamental law of active management (FLOAM).

For example:

Identify the key components (i.e., breadth and the information coefficient) of the FLOAM

- The breadth of a strategy is the number of independent active bets placed into an active portfolio
- The information coefficient measures managerial skill as the correlation between managerial return predictions and realized returns

Describe how the FLOAM can be used to understand changes in the information ratio

- The FLOAM connects breadth and skill to the information ratio
- Information Ratio = Information coefficient $* \sqrt{Breadth}$
- The Information coefficient measures managerial skill as the correlation between managerial return predictions and realized returns

Recognize trade-offs involved in changing or maintaining the information ratio

- There is a trade-off between breadth and the information coefficient
- It is generally not possible for an active manager to increase breadth without decreasing the IC at the same time

Define non-active bets and recognize their role in the FLOAM

- Non-active bets are added to keep the active manager's return from straying too much from the benchmark
- As a result, the breadth of the portfolio may be much less than the number of positions

16.4 Demonstrate knowledge of approaches to implementing anomaly strategies.

For example:

Recognize methods for integrating anomalies using factor models

- To integrate a set of anomalies into a single trading signal, the manager assigns scores to each stock based on each anomaly
- Most quantitative managers use multiple-factor scoring models and combine the factor scores into a single trading signal

Define pairs trading and describe the steps involved in constructing the portfolio

- Portfolio is constructed by going long in the underpriced security and short in the overpriced security

Discuss the effect of short selling on reducing risk and increasing alpha

- Greater breadth via short selling increases the risk-return profile

Describe the limits to arbitrage and their effect on market efficiency and investment strategies

- Some markets restrict short selling
- Limits to arbitrage can negatively impact investment strategies

16.5 Demonstrate knowledge of the three major strategies of equity hedge funds.

For example:

Describe the key characteristics of short-bias hedge funds

- Net short position in the stock market
- Expected to rise very little or even decline in an efficient market since markets tend to rise over time
- Should be evaluated on performance relative to their negative systematic risk

Recognize inferences that can be drawn from comparing definable characteristics of short-bias hedge funds with their historical stand-alone and portfolio performance

- Slightly outperformed equities between 2000-10 with higher volatility
- Very high negative correlation to the market

Describe the key characteristics of equity long/short hedge funds

- Combines a core group of long stock positions with short positions in stocks or index options & futures
- Come in two varieties: fundamental and quantitative

Recognize inferences that can be drawn from comparing definable characteristics of equity long/short hedge funds with their historical standalone and portfolio performance

- Performed better than the overall equity market but not as well as bonds in terms of risk and return

Describe the key characteristics of equity market-neutral hedge funds

- Establishes both long and short positions
- Positions are designed to neutralize *overall* equity market risk
- Funds may exhibit mean neutrality and variance neutrality
- Some use leverage

Recognize inferences that can be drawn from comparing definable characteristics of equity market-neutral funds with their historical stand-alone and portfolio performance

- The strategy has extremely low volatility and generates an attractive Sharpe ratio
- Consistent positive correlation with commodities and negative correlation to equities

Chapter 17: Funds of Hedge Funds

Keywords

Access: An investor's ability to place new or increased money in a particular fund.

Funds of funds: Funds with a portfolio of hedge funds rather than investing directly in stocks, bonds or other securities.

Investable index: An index of security prices that reflects returns that can be generated in practice with an actual investment program.

Liquidity facility: A standby agreement with a major bank to provide temporary cash for specified needs with pre-specified conditions.

Seeding funds: Funds of funds that invest in newly created individual hedge funds.

Self-selection effect: Where only the most successful and confident single-strategy hedge fund managers choose to become multi-strategy managers by hiring a team of experts and expanding into the world of multi-strategy funds.

Learning Objectives

17.1 Demonstrate knowledge of the benefits and costs of diversification in hedge fund investing.

For example:

Recognize how indices can serve as valuable tools in constructing hedge fund portfolios and analyzing portfolio performance

- An investor can replicate an index by owning the underlying securities or using derivatives

Identify and evaluate six methods by which investors can obtain or approximate the returns of a well-diversified hedge fund portfolio

- Build and invest in a portfolio of investments in individual hedge fund managers
- Invest with one or more multistrategy funds
- Invest in a fund of funds
- Invest in a structured product with hedge funds or fund of funds
- Invest in investable indices through firms offering hedge funds that mimic the hedge fund index
- Invest in replication products

Discuss the relationship between the number of funds in a portfolio and the level of diversification

- Fothergill and Coke found that a portfolio of 15-20 hedge funds can reduce portfolio volatility to the level of fixed income investments

Describe the process for identifying funds for an institutional portfolio or fund of funds

- Start with the hedge fund universe of 7,000 funds
- Can start screening hedge fund databases with over 4,000 hedge funds
- Quantitative screens can funnel the process down to 500 to 1,000 funds
- Due diligence can funnel the process down to 100 to 200 funds; most expensive and challenging part of the process
- Fund of funds: 10 to 50 funds

Recognize the costs involved in building a hedge fund portfolio with internal staff

- Subscribing to hedge fund databases
- Hire and retain internal staff
- Expenses associated with visiting and evaluating managers

17.2 Demonstrate knowledge of investing in multi-strategy funds.

For example:

Evaluate fee related advantages of multi-strategy funds

- The advantage of multi-strategy funds over fund of funds is the lack of a second level of fees

- The second level of fees can cause fund of funds to have total fees of 3 and 30

Evaluate flexibility and transparency in the context of multi-strategy funds

- Multi-strategy funds have greater flexibility to make tactical strategy allocation and risk management decisions than fund of funds
- When a fund of funds manager invests with underlying managers, each investment is subject to possible liquidity terms and limited transparency
- With a multi-strategy approach, the portfolio manager has real-time access and transparency to all positions
- The multi-strategy manager can also direct trading teams to reduce or expand portfolios

Evaluate potential advantages related to manager selection and operational risk management by funds of funds

- Funds of funds managers may have a greater ability to add value through manager selection than multi-strategy funds
- While asset allocation is more important than manager selection with traditional investments, the opposite is true for hedge funds
- Operational risk is spread out with in a fund of funds portfolio

17.3 Demonstrate knowledge of the process of investing in funds of hedge funds.

For example:

Identify advantages that funds of funds have over direct hedge fund investments

- Diversification
- Professional management
- Reduced operational risk

Discuss empirical evidence regarding fund of funds returns and the potential for reduced biases in reported performance

- Funds of funds returns have generally lagged the returns of the overall hedge fund index
- Funds of funds give a less biased view of hedge fund performance for the following reasons:
    o Funds of funds that invested in funds that eventually liquidated retain the returns in those funds in their records – reduced survivor bias
    o Funds of funds tally hedge fund returns from the date they are invested – reduced instant history bias
    o Funds of funds use actual investment weights that may better reflect the weights used by typical investors

Recognize the varying investment objectives of funds of hedge funds

- Seeking returns that are uncorrelated to stock and bond markets with lower downside risk

Describe how funds of funds can act as venture capitalists

- Some funds of funds are seeding funds and invest in start-up hedge funds

17.4 Demonstrate knowledge of historical performance of funds of hedge funds.

For example:

Recognize inferences that can be drawn from comparing definable characteristics of market-defensive funds of funds with their historical standalone and portfolio performance

- Market defensive funds have underlying and unhedged short positions
- Near zero kurtosis and skewness
- Positive correlation to commodities and global bonds

Recognize inferences that can be drawn from comparing definable characteristics of conservative funds of funds with their historical stand-alone and portfolio performance

- Conservative funds have underlying hedged positions
- Extremely negative skewness with high kurtosis
- Low volatility

Recognize inferences that can be drawn from comparing definable characteristics of strategic funds of funds with their historical stand-alone and portfolio performance

- Strategic funds of funds tend to have underlying directional bets and invest in funds with more opportunistic strategies
- Moderate negative skewness and kurtosis
- High correlation to equities and moderate volatility

Recognize inferences that can be drawn from comparing definable characteristics of diversified funds of funds with their historical stand-alone and portfolio performance

- Diversified funds of funds invest in a variety of strategies among multiple managers
- Returns mirror composite fund of funds index
- Negative skewness, positive kurtosis

Topic 5: Commodities

Chapter 18: Commodity Futures Pricing

Keywords

Arbitrage: Buying and selling the same instrument in two different markets in an attempt to make a riskless profit.

Arbitrage-free model: A financial engineering model that assigns prices to derivatives or other instruments in such a way that it is impossible to construct arbitrages between two or more of those prices. For example, if an option pricing formula assigned prices to put and call options that violated put-call parity, that would not be an arbitrage-free model.

Backwardation: Market condition wherein the price of a forward or futures contract is trading below the expected spot price at contract maturity. The resulting futures or forward curve would typically be downward sloping (i.e. "inverted"), since contracts for further dates would typically trade at even lower prices.

Basis (in a forward contract): The difference between the spot price of the referenced asset and the price of a forward contract.

Calendar spread: The price difference between futures or forward prices on the same underlying asset that differ only by settlement date.

Contango: Market condition wherein the price of a forward or futures contract is trading above the expected spot price at contract maturity. The futures or forward curve would typically be upward sloping (i.e. "normal"), since contracts for further dates would typically trade at even higher prices.

Convenience yield: The economic benefit that the holder of an inventory in the commodity receives from directly holding the inventory rather than having a long position in a forward contract on the commodity. The value of physical ownership of a commodity rather than synthetic ownership since physical ownership enables more immediate and certain ability to use the asset for an intended purpose. A jewelry manufacturer benefits from having physical gold in its inventory to protect from supply disruptions.

Cost-of-carry: Cost of storing a physical commodity, such as grain or metals, over a period of time.

Deferred contracts: Futures contracts that settle in months beyond the closest current trading month (contracts with longer times to settlement).

Financed positions: Positions that enable the economic ownership of an asset without the posting of the purchase price (e.g., forward contracts).

Forward contract: Private agreement to trade underlying asset in the future at agreed price today.

Futures contract: Standardized forward contract that trades on an exchange.

Inelastic supply: A market situation in which any increase or decrease in the price of a good or service does not result in a corresponding increase or decrease in its supply.

Initial margin: Amount required to be collateralized in order to open a margin position.

Maintenance margin: Amount required to be kept in collateral until the margin position is closed (on an ongoing basis).

Margin call: A demand by a broker that a customer deposit enough to bring his margin up to the minimum requirement caused by the decline in market prices (or marking-to-market of losses) of a security or commodity purchased on margin.

Marked-to-market: Also known as fair value accounting this practice refers to accounting for the "fair value" of an asset or liability based on the current market price. Mark-to-market accounting can change values on the balance sheet as market conditions change. In contrast, historical cost accounting, based on the past transactions, is simpler, more stable, and easier to perform, but does not represent current market value. One side of the futures contracts benefits from a price change and receives cash from the other side throughout a contract's life.

Nearby contract: Among several different futures contracts, the one with the shortest maturity.

Normal backwardation: see 'Backwardation'

Normal contango: See 'Contango'.

Open interest: Refers to the total number of derivative contracts, like futures and options, that have not been settled in the immediately previous time period for a specific underlying security. A large open interest indicates more activity and liquidity for the contract.

Perfectly elastic supply: Where supply is infinite at any one price.

Rolling contracts: Trading out of a standard contract and then buying the contract with next longest maturity, so as to maintain a position with constant maturity.

Spot market: Public financial market, in which financial instruments or commodities are traded for immediate delivery.

Spot price: The current price at which a particular security can be bought or sold at a specified time and place.

Storage costs: Part of the futures cost of carry along with insurance and interest on the invested funds. Storage costs of commodities include warehouse fees, insurance, transportation and spoilage.

Swap: Agreement to exchange payments of periodic cash flows that depend on future asset prices or interest rates.

Term structure of forward prices: Refers to the price curve formed by the prices of forward contracts over various expiration months.

The law of one price: An economic law that in an efficient market, all identical goods must have only one price.

Variation margin: Additional funds that a broker may request from a client so that the initial margin requirements of his position keep up with any losses.

Learning Objectives

18.1 Demonstrate knowledge of forward and futures contracts.

For example:

Describe the differences between forward and futures contracts

	Forward	**Futures**
Traded	OTC	Exchange
Contract structure	Customized	Standardized
Marked-to-market	No	Yes
Counterparty risk	Greater	Less

Describe and apply initial margin to futures positions

- The initial margin is the collateral deposit made at the initiation of a long or short futures position
- The buyer of the contract must have the initial margin available as collateral in order to establish the position

Describe marking-to-market of futures positions

- The side of a futures contract that benefits from a price change receives cash from the counterparty throughout the contract's life, resulting in a zero market value of the derivative after being marked-to-market

Describe and apply maintenance margins to futures positions

- After initiation, market participants are subject to maintenance margins which are minimum collateral requirements imposed on an ongoing basis until the position is closed
- If the collateral falls below the maintenance margin requirement due to marking-to-market of loses, a margin call is issued at which point the market participant is required to deposit additional collateral
- If the investor cannot meet the margin call, the broker can liquidate positions in the account

18.2 Demonstrate knowledge of the roll process of futures contracts.

For example:

Explain the process of creating and maintaining long-term futures exposures through short-term futures positions

- Unlike equities, you can't just simply buy and hold futures contracts
- Long-term exposure is maintained by rolling over short-term futures positions

Discuss the effects of rollover decisions on the returns of long-term futures exposures

- Decisions made on when to roll over contracts and the duration of contracts to roll into will affect long-run returns

18.3 Demonstrate knowledge of the term structure of forward prices and the pricing models of futures and forward prices.

For example:

Explain the term structure of forward prices

- The relationship between forward prices and the time to delivery
- Term structure can also be viewed for forward rates

Explain arbitrage-free models

- An arbitrage-free model of spot gold prices in different currencies implies that gold should trade at the same prices globally when adjusted for exchange rates

Describe various shapes that the term structure of futures prices can assume

- Flat – consistent with zero interest rates, no dividends or costs (e.g., storage)
- Contango – upward sloping
- Backwardation - downward sloping
- Non-flat term structures are due to carrying costs

Understand and apply the cost-of-carry model

- Any financial difference between maintaining a position in the cash market and maintaining a position in the futures market
- Cost-of-carry models identify two strategies with identical payoffs and attribute the differences in current prices to differences in the costs of carrying each strategy
- The total cost of carrying the asset ownership using the cash market must equal the cost of the forward position (which has no extra costs)
- Spot price + carrying costs = forward price

Benefits and costs of direct asset ownership

	Real assets	**Financial assets**
Benefits	Convenience (y)	Dividends and coupons (d)
Costs	Interest (r), storage (c)	Interest (r), custody

Describe and apply arbitrage-free pricing models of financial forward prices

- Direct asset ownership requires an investment of cash (or borrowing of funds) while forward contracts require zero investment (except posting collateral, which is interest-bearing)
- A long position in an forward contract on an equity index is identical to a long position in the equity index and that is financed through borrowing (a short position in a bond)

- The long position in a forward contract does not receive the cash flows from the underlying asset (e.g., dividends, coupons) and therefore the forward price is lowered

Forward Price = $S*e^{(Rf-d)T}$ = Spot Price * $e^{(\text{continuously compounded Rf – dividend or coupon rate}) * T \text{ maturity}}$

Describe and apply arbitrage-free pricing models of forward contracts on physical assets

- Physical assets such as commodities typically involve storage costs and convenience yields
- Forward Price = Spot Price * $e^{(\text{Rf + storage costs – dividends \& coupons – convenience yield})}$ = $S * e^{(r+c-d-y)T}$

Discuss the effect of elasticity, demand shifts, and supply shifts on the term structure of forward prices

- Commodity forward contracts face greater complexities since unlike financial forward contracts commodity forwards prices are determined by forecasts of supply and demand
- Agricultural commodity supply if often harvested annually so is rather inelastic (supplies change slowly in response to market prices) while currency supply is elastic (any quantity demanded can be instantaneously and limitlessly supplied without changes in the market price)
- When the supply of a commodity cannot respond quickly to meet changing demand, its convenience yield is likely to be higher, since users of the commodity will have a greater fear of shortages
- When demand can change quickly, the convenience yield is likely to be higher, since users of the commodity will have a greater fear of shortages

Discuss the potential barriers to implementing arbitrage strategies in physical commodity markets

- Physical commodities that offer a convenience yield and inelastic supplies tend to be difficult to borrow because entities that own the commodities do not want to lend them at little or no cost
- Spot prices can be a lot higher than forward prices in these markets

18.4 Demonstrate knowledge of the concepts of backwardation, normal backwardation, contango, and normal contango.

For example:

Discuss backwardation and contango in an efficient market

- Backwardation and contango reflect the cost of carry in an efficient market
- A long position in a forward contract in a backwardated market is no more attractive than a long position in a contango market (returns for both markets can be equal) unless the slope of the term structure of forward prices is driven by market inefficiencies
- If d>r, term structure would be downward sloping while it would be upward sloping for r>d; however, the returns would be equal in a case where the dividends are reinvested into growth for one investment and paid out to investors for the other

Explain the relationships between forward prices and spot prices under normal backwardation and normal contango

- In an efficient market, forward prices must differ from expected spot prices whenever the position involves systematic risk
- Normal backwardation
  - Forward price < expected spot price
  - Expected profit could be due to compensation for bearing risk
- Normal contango
  - Forward price > expected spot price
  - In an efficient market, normal contango would only exist for commodity forwards with negative betas – rare

Discuss expected returns to spot positions and forward positions (long and short) under normal backwardation and normal contango

- Normal backwardation : a *long* forward contract is expected to make a profit
- Normal contango: a *short* forward contract is expected to make a profit

18.5 Demonstrate knowledge of the characteristics of returns on forward and futures contracts.

For example:

Discuss the potential of futures and forward contracts as sources of ex ante alpha and/or beta

- Futures and forward contracts may be used as beta drivers or alpha drivers
- A forward contract on a stock index and be a cost-effective way to attain beta
- An investor using these contracts as an alpha driver might see the forward contracts on a commodity as mispriced relative to the underlying spot price

Discuss the relationship between ex ante alpha and the shape of the term structure of forward prices

- Ex ante alpha exists when the term structure of forward prices takes on a shape that is informationally inefficient (don't reflect available information)
- Investors can exploit by being long in underpriced contracts and short positions in overpriced contracts and generate ex ante alpha

Discuss the basis of forward contracts, calendar spreads, and trading strategies involving hedging futures exposures using positions in spot or futures contracts of different maturity

- Basis = spot price – forward price
- A position that is short the forward contract and long the spot price is riskless and has an expected return equal to the cost of carry
- Calendar spread trading focuses on the search for mispriced futures or forward contracts on the same commodity that differ by settlement date

Chapter 19: Commodities: Applications and Evidence

Keywords

Basis risk: Spot returns differ from futures or forward returns due to basis risk, or the risk associated with changes in the relationship between spot and futures prices.

Also the risk that offsetting investments in a hedging strategy will not experience price changes in entirely opposite directions from each other. It is the risk associated with imperfect hedging using futures.

Collateral yield: Return on cash used as margin to take long derivatives exposure. Typically a T-bill return.

Excess return: The return generated from changes in futures prices (and ignoring collateral yield).

Inflation: A rise in the general level of prices of goods and services in an economy over a period of time or the decline in the value of money relative to the value of a general bundle of goods and services.

Inflation risk: The uncertainty over the future real value (after inflation) of your investment.

Market weight: The percentage of the total market portfolio attributable to each asset in the portfolio.

Roll return: See 'Roll Yield.'

Roll yield: Yield that a futures investor captures when their futures contract converges to the spot price; in a backwardated futures market the roll yield is positive, whereas when the market is in contango the roll yield is negative.

Spot return: The return on the underlying asset in the spot market.

Learning Objectives

19.1 Demonstrate knowledge of the diversification benefits of commodities .

For example:

Explain the sources of potential diversification benefits offered by commodities

- Commodity prices are not directly determined by the discounted value of future cash flows and changes in market discount rates but are determined by supply & demand; thus, they are driven by different economic fundamentals than stocks and bonds and should have little or even negative correlation
- Positive correlation with inflation (stocks and bonds tend to be negatively correlate with inflation)
- They react differently (from stocks and bonds) at different parts of the business cycle
- Commodities are a major cost of corporate production, so as commodities prices increase corporate profits will fall causing stocks and bonds to decline (with the exception of commodity-producing firms)

Discuss commodities in the context of equilibrium diversification

- Based on CAPM, the issue in determining appropriate exposure to each commodity is in determining the market weight of that commodity because determining the total global market value of a commodity is challenging

Discuss how market imperfections relate to determining allocations to commodities

- Markets are imperfect and could remain out of equilibrium for extended periods of time due to taxes or transaction costs
- Shortages and oversupplies of commodities are not quickly corrected through price mechanisms
- Theory is unable to prescribe optimal portfolio allocations in imperfect markets and in markets in disequilibrium

Discuss commodities as a diversifier of inflation risk

- Commodity prices are an important determinant of the price indices that measure inflation

19.2 Demonstrate knowledge of commodities as potential return enhancers.

For example:

Discuss potential return enhancement from idiosyncratic returns

- Generating alpha through commodity exposure is based on the investor's belief that the underlying commodity itself is inefficiently priced

Discuss potential return enhancement from systematic returns in efficient markets

- Commodities can offer superior returns due to their systematic risks

- Due to their inflation-hedging capabilities and their likely protection from downside risk, the systematic risks of commodities should theoretically be low (and so should their returns) if they are efficiently priced

Discuss potential return enhancement from systematic returns in inefficient markets

- The potential for high returns through beta exposure may occur in some commodities and not in others based on supply & demand factors

19.3 Demonstrate knowledge of investing in commodities without futures.

For example:

Recognize direct investments in physical commodities

- Storage and transportation costs make owning physical commodities undesirable
- Some market participants have a competitive advantage to holding the commodity (convenience yield)

Recognize investments in commodities through related equity instruments

- An investor can gain commodity exposure by owning securities of a firm that sells commodities (e.g., a natural resource company)
- However, operating risks and equity market risk are introduced

Recognize investments in commodities through exchange-traded funds (ETFs)

- ETFs can invest in futures markets, equity markets, physical ownership

Recognize investments in commodities through commodity linked notes

- Commodity linked notes are fixed income securities whose value at maturity is based on an underlying commodity (or basket)
- Typically structured products created via financial engineering to have commodity exposure through commodity derivatives
- Also issued by commodity-producing firms to match the risks of its assets and liabilities
- Advantages:
  - The investor doesn't have to worry about rolling over the contract, as in futures (for the issuer to worry about)
  - Benefits of being a debt instrument for entities that may not be allowed to take on direct commodities exposure (e.g., pensions)

Apply option valuation methods to commodity linked notes

- Incorporate appreciation and coupons to calculate the expected payoff

19.4 Demonstrate knowledge of commodity investment through futures contracts.

For example:

Recognize the basis risk and investments in commodities through futures contracts

- The returns to investing in a particular commodity futures contract can differ from returns in the underlying due:
  - The costs of carry for the spot position not being equal to the costs implied by the basis
  - Basis changes (risk associated with the changes in the relationship between spot and futures prices)
- Returns in forwards/futures with different settlement dates can differ due to:
  - Calendar spread
  - Exposures are long-term and rolled over with different costs

Recognize and apply various components of returns to futures positions (i.e., spot return, roll yield, collateral yield, and excess return)

- Spot return: The return on the underlying asset in the spot market
- Roll yield: The portion of the return of a futures position from the change in the contract's basis through time.
- Collateral yield: The interest earned from the riskless bonds used to collateralize the futures contract. Partial collateralization generates leveraged returns.
- Excess return: The return generated from changes in futures prices.

Discuss and explain roll yield (roll return) for financial and physical commodity futures

- The basis of a futures contract changes for two reasons:
  - As time passes, the time to settlement of the futures contract shortens and the contract's price rolls up or down toward the spot price
  - As components of the cost of carry vary (interest rates, dividend yield, storage costs, convenience yield) so does the basis as it depends on those four determinants

Discuss convergence and the relationship between futures and spot prices through time

- As time passes, the time to settlement of the futures contract shortens and the contract's price rolls up or down toward the spot price
- Futures positions held to settlement generate the same returns as spot positions when adjusted for financing and other costs of carry

Recognize rollover strategies and their effect on returns from futures investments

- The differences between the returns of various rollover strategies are equal to the returns of calendar spreads

19.5 Demonstrate knowledge of fallacies with regards to roll return.

For example:

Discuss three common fallacies associated with the concept of roll return

- Roll return is directly generated by closing one position and opening a new position

- o Roll return is NOT the difference in price between the contract that is closed and the contract that is opened during a rollover
  - o Roll return occurs throughout the time that a contract is held
  - o Roll return is the difference between the price at which a contract is opened and the price that the same contract is closed *in excess of* the return on a spot commodity position
- Roll return is always positive in backwardated markets
  - o If costs of carry change, there's no guarantee that roll return will be positive
  - o It is positive for the term structure of forward prices to shift
- Positive roll return guarantees superior returns (alpha)
  - o Roll return can be positive when there is a high dividend or coupon rate on the underlying asset
  - o Owning a forward contract on a financial asset offers the benefit of avoiding the finance cost and the disadvantage of losing the dividend yield
  - o Virtually all futures contracts offer roll return and the mere presence of it does not indicate alpha
  - o Alpha may exist when there are market imperfections and inefficiencies via storage costs and convenience yields

19.6 Demonstrate knowledge of commodity indices.

For example:

Discuss properties of commodity indices

- A commodity index should represent the total return that would be earned from holding long-only positions in unleveraged physical commodity futures
- Financial futures are not included since they are directly linked to the price of the underlying assets
- Since spot prices of physical commodities vary between locations, true changes in physical commodity prices are better measured with indices based on the prices of futures contracts

Discuss the characteristics of three popular commodity indices (i.e., S&PGSCI, DJ-UBSCI, and CRB)

- S&P GSCI
  - o Standard & Poor's Goldman Sachs Commodity Index
  - o Composed of the first nearby futures contract in each commodity
  - o Investors can by a future based on this index
  - o Weighting based on 5-yr averages of each commodity's contribution to world production
- DJ-UBSCI
  - o Dow Jones UBS Commodity Index
  - o Composed of futures contracts on 20 physical commodities
  - o Weighting is based on liquidity data
  - o Primarily trading activity weighted
- CRB
  - o Reuters/Jefferies Commodity Research Bureau
  - o Oldest commodity index

- o Made up of 19 commodities quoted on the NYMEX, CBOT, LME, CME, and COMEX
- o Follows a more subjective and fixed weighting scheme based on tiers

19.7 Demonstrate knowledge of risks associated with commodity investments.

For example:

Discuss the effect of event risk on returns from investments in commodities

- Commodities tend to benefit from events since surprises that occur in commodities markets tend to unexpectedly reduce the supply of the commodity to the market
- Commodity are likely to be uncorrelated with each other and with the equity markets (sometimes negatively correlated to equities)

Discuss the role of commodities as defensive investments

- Commodities are market neutral and sometimes even benefit from market turmoil
- Commodities help reduce downside risk

Discuss acceptance of commodity investments by institutional investors

- As institutions seek greater diversification to their portfolios, commodity investing is growing to meet demand

19.8 Demonstrate knowledge of the return characteristics of commodity investments.

For example:

Recognize inferences that can be drawn from comparing definable characteristics of commodities with their historical stand-alone and portfolio performance

- Diversification benefits
- Highly correlated to equities during extreme market events

Topic 6: Private Equity

Chapter 20: Introduction to Private Equity

Keywords

Charge-off loans: Loans of a financial institution or other lender that have been sold to investors and written off the books of the lender at a loss.

Conversion price: The issue price of a convertible bond divided by the conversion ratio.

Conversion ratio: The number of common shares for which a convertible bond can be exchanged.

Covenants: Terms in debt contracts that either require certain actions of the borrower (affirmative covenants) or restrict certain actions (negative covenants).

Cov-lite loans: Loan agreements which do not contain the usual protective covenants for the benefit of the lending party. Seen as more risky because it removes the early warning signs lenders would otherwise receive through traditional covenants.

Distressed debt investing: Investing in distressed securities (securities of companies or government entities that are either already in default, under bankruptcy protection, or in distress and heading toward such a condition).

Equity kicker: Loan agreement under which a lender agrees to charge lower than normal interest rates in return for a share of ownership (equity) in the property or business for which loan is advanced.

Haircut: Percentage discount that's applied informally to the market value of a stock or the face value of a bond in an attempt to account for the risk of loss that the investment poses.

Incurrence covenants: Incurrence covenants are tested for a specific event, such as when a borrower wishes to take out more debt. They typically require a borrower to take or not take a specific action once a specified event occurs.

Junk bonds: Bonds rated below investment grade.

Leveraged buyouts (LBOs): Acquisition (usually of a company, but can also be single assets such as a real estate property) where the purchase price is financed through a combination of equity and significant debt and in which the cash flows or assets of the target are used to secure and repay the debt.

Leveraged loans: Loans extended to companies or individuals that already have considerable amounts of debt (non-investment grade debt). Lenders consider leveraged loans to carry a higher risk of default.

Maintenance covenants: Maintenance covenants are tested regularly -- often as frequently as every three months -- and are common for heavily indebted companies, for example companies bought out by private equity firms using leverage. They are stricter than incurrence covenants in that they require a standard to be regularly met in order to avoid default.

Management buyouts: Form of acquisition where a company's existing managers acquire a large part or all of the company from either the parent company or from the private owners.

Merchant banking: When financial institutions buy nonfinancial companies for potential profits as opposed to acquiring or merging with other banks.

Mezzanine debt: Form of private equity in the form of high-interest debt with potential equity participation.

Middle market: Smaller firms with a market cap between $200 million and $2 billion.

Negative covenants: Terms in debt contracts that restrict certain actions (e.g. restriction from paying dividends).

Positive covenants: Terms in debt contracts that either require certain actions of the borrower (e.g. maintain a certain debt ratio).

Private equity firms: Private investment firms that invest in companies that are not publicly traded.

Private equity funds: Funds that invest in companies that are not publicly traded.

Private investments in public equity (PIPE): Involves the selling of publicly traded common shares or some form of preferred stock or convertible security to private investors and is exempt from registration. It is the allocation of shares not through a public offering in a stock exchange. PIPE deals are part of the primary market.

Prudent person standard: A requirement that specifies levels of care that should be exercised in particular decision-making roles, such as investment decisions made by a fiduciary.

Segmentation: The idea that there are limited numbers of participants who focus on specific aspects and activities of a market, rather than varying their range of activities more broadly throughout all available opportunities.

Story credit: Debt with credit risk based on unusual circumstances.

Structured PIPEs: A PIPE that issues convertible debt (common or preferred shares).

Syndicated: Refers to the use of a group of entities in underwriting a security offering.

Toxic PIPE: A PIPE may dilute existing shareholders' equity ownership, particularly if the seller has agreed to provide the investors with downside protections against market price declines (a death spiral), which can lead to issuance of more shares to the PIPE investors for no more money.

Traditional PIPEs: A traditional PIPE is one in which stock, either common or preferred, is issued at a set/fixed price to raise capital for the issuer.

Underlying business enterprises: The underlying businesses invested in by the private equity firm.

Venture capital: Financial capital provided to early-stage, high-potential, high risk, growth startup companies.

Vintage year: The year a private equity fund commences operations. The year in which the first influx of investment capital is delivered to a project or company.

Learning Objectives

20.1 Demonstrate knowledge of private equity terminology.

For example:

Recognize the structure of private equity funds and investments / Explain the roles of various entities involved in private equity investments

- Institutional investors are LPs
- Private equity firms are GPs
- They both invest in the private equity fund which in turn invests in underlying businesses

20.2 Demonstrate knowledge of the major forms of private equity investments that involve direct ownership of equity.

For example:

Recognize characteristics of venture capital investment and its role in business startups

- Represents senior equity stakes in firms that are still privately owned and illiquid
- 5-10 year investment horizon
- VCs often provide managerial guidance and control

Recognize characteristics of leveraged buyouts and the role of debt in these transactions

- Debt financing (bank loans or newly issued bonds) is used to take a company private
- D/E ratio much higher after the acquisition

Recognize characteristics of management buyouts

- A way for management to own the company using an LBO

Recognize characteristics of merchant banking and the benefits it offers to financial institutions

- Units within financial institutions that buy and sell nonfinancial companies for the profits that they can generate
- Merchant banks also allow the bank to leverage its relationship with the buyout company into other money-generating businesses

20.3 Demonstrate knowledge of the major forms of private equity that involve direct ownership of debt securities.

For example:

Describe mezzanine debt and explain why it is considered to be a type of private equity investment

- It's considered to be a type of private equity investment due to its high risk and because it often comes with equity participation (equity kicker)

Recognize the role of mezzanine debt as a source of funding in private equity transactions

- Mezzanine financing is used for transitional periods in a company rather than to fund day-to-day operations
- Story credits

Describe distressed debt securities

- The practice of buying debt of companies that have already defaulted on their debt, may be on the brink of default, or maybe seeking bankruptcy protection
- Debt often trades for pennies on the dollar

Explain the factors that have contributed to the growth of the market for distressed debt securities

- Many more types of nontraditional loans became available for sale
- Growth of covenant-light loans
- Many banks are applying active risk management and selling nonperforming and subperforming loans into the market at large discounts to remove them from their books

Explain various types of debt covenants

- Positive and negative covenants
- Incurrence covenants
- Maintenance covenants

Describe leverage loan securities and factors contributing to their growth

- Leverage loan securities are syndicated bank loans to non-investment grade borrowers
- Growth has been driven by:
  - The development and expansion of their secondary market
  - An active secondary market has encouraged banks to issue loans and motivated institutions to invest in the loans

20.4 Demonstrate knowledge of trends and innovations in private equity markets.

For example:

Discuss secondary markets in the context of private equity

- A private equity investor may need to sell part of a portfolio

Explain private investment in public equity (PIPE) transactions and compare them to other private equity investments

- The securities are sold directly to investors who cannot trade them in a secondary market for a period of time
- This way, an issuing company can quickly raise capital without the need for a lengthy registration process

- PIPEs allow private equity firms to gain a significant stake in a company at a discount

Describe advantages that PIPEs offer investors

- The greater the illiquidity (it's privately placed), the greater the discount on the PIPE's issue price
- An investor can acquire a large block of stock at a discount

Describe various types of PIPEs and the purposes for their creation and use

- Structured PIPEs
- Toxic PIPEs

Discuss hedge fund participation in private equity

- Diversification
- Desire to apply skills in new areas
- More favorable fee structure

Contrast private equity funds and hedge funds

	Private equity	Hedge funds
Incentive fees	Collected at deal termination; based on realized values; collected at exits	Front loaded; based on changes in NAV; collected on a regular basis (quarterly, etc.)
Investor capital	Do not distribute incentive fees until the original investor capital has been repaid	Does not need to be returned first to collect incentive fees
Management Clawback of incentive fees	Typically required when profits are followed by losses	None
Hurdle rate	Usually used	Used rarely
Deal terms	Less favorable	More favorable

Chapter 21: Equity Types of Private Equity

Keywords

20-bagger: An investment which is worth twenty times its original purchase price.

Angel investing: An affluent individual who provides capital for a business start-up, usually in exchange for convertible debt or ownership equity.

Auction process: A process that involves bidding among several private equity buyers with the deal going to the highest bidder.

Business plan: Formal statement of a set of business goals, the reasons they are believed attainable, and the plan for reaching those goals.

Buy-and-build: LBO value creation strategy that involves combining several operating companies or divisions through additional buyouts.

Buyout-to-buyout: When a private equity firm sells one of its portfolio companies to another private equity firm.

Capital calls: Legal right of an investment firm to demand a portion of the money promised to it by an investor. Also known as a draw down or a capital commitment.

Clawback provision: The provision for when the GP must return incentive fees already paid.

Club deal: Refers to a leveraged buyout or other private equity investment that involves several different private equity investment firms.

Committed capital: A contractual agreement between an investor and a private equity fund that obligates the investor to contribute money to the fund.

Compound option: An option on an option.

Conglomerates: Combination of two or more corporations engaged in entirely different businesses that fall under one corporate group, usually involving a parent company and many subsidiaries.

Efficiency buyouts: LBOs that improve operating efficiency.

Entrepreneurship: The act of starting and running new enterprises.

Escrow agreement: Where a portion of the manager's incentive fees are held in a segregated account until the entire fund is liquidated.

Exit plan: When VC firms liquidate their investment in the start-up company to realize a gain for themselves and their investors.

First- or early-stage venture capital: The start-up company should have a viable product that has been beta tested in order to receive this form of capital.

Gearing: Increasing risk through leverage (debt).

Limited liability: Concept whereby a person's financial liability is limited to a fixed sum, most commonly the value of a person's investment in a company or partnership.

Mezzanine stage: Refers to a later stage investment provided to a company that is already producing and selling a product or service, for the purpose of helping the company achieve a critical objective that, in many cases, will enable it to go public.

Second- or late-stage/expansion: At this point, the start-up may have generated its first profitable quarter or is soon to break even.

Seed capital: The first stage where VC firms invest their own capital.

Sourcing investments: The second stage in the life cycle of a VC fund that involves locating potential investments.

Turnaround strategies: LBO funds that look for underperforming companies with excessive debt and poor management.

Venture capital: Support via equity financing to start-up companies unable to attract capital from traditional sources such as banks or public capital markets.

Learning Objectives

21.1 Demonstrate knowledge of the relationships between venture capital and leveraged buyouts.

For example:

Recognize the role of venture capital and leverage buyouts as sources of funding for corporations through their life cycle

- VC and LBOs are at the opposite ends of the life cycle of a company
- VC – start-up companies
- LBO – mature, more established companies

21.2 Demonstrate knowledge of the underlying businesses (portfolio companies) of venture capital.

For example:

Recognize characteristics of businesses underlying venture capital investment

- VC funds typically invest convertible preferred stock into start-ups because it is senior to common in terms of dividends, voting rights and liquidation
- VC funds may also invest convertible notes and debentures

Describe the role of business plans and exit plans in venture capital investment

- Business plans are the most important document that VCs use to determine whether or not to invest
- The business plans objectives are to secure VC financing and provide an internal game plan for the start-up company's development
- Facilitating exit strategies is another way that a VC can add value to the start-up founders

21.3 Demonstrate knowledge of venture capital funds.

For example:

Recognize how venture capital fund managers raise capital

- VC funds are typically structured as limited partnerships with the VC firm as the GP

Recognize the structure of venture capital funds and the roles played by various entities

- GPs are typically restricted in the amount of private investments the fund manager can make on its own and in their ability to sell their partnership interest to a third party
- GPs are also restricted in the amount of future fund raising and also are generally limited or restricted from having outside interests

Describe and apply typical venture capital fund fees

- Management fee is assessed on the amount of committed capital, not invested capital

Describe the stages of the life cycle of venture capital funds and portfolio companies

- Investors in VC funds will see their accounting value of their investment drop over the first 3-5 years due to the organization fees and the fact that well-performing investments will not show gains until exits are achieved (J-curve effect)
- Stages of VC funds
    - 1. Fund raising – capital is committed, not collected
    - 2. Sourcing investments
    - 3. Investment of capital
    - 4. Operation and management of portfolio companies – Begins after all the funds have been invested and last almost to the end of the term of the fund
    - 5. Windup and liquidation – The fund is in the harvesting stage and exits are achieved (e.g., IPO, strategic sale, etc.)

Explain the importance of financing stages in distinguishing among various venture capital funds

- Some VC funds provide first-stage or seed capital while others invest in companies that are further along
- Angel investing: Usually friends and family and at this stage and maybe an angel investor
- Seed capital: This phase of financing usually raises $1M to $5M to complete product development or begin marketing; company may be generating a little revenue but is likely to be unprofitable at this stage
- First or early-stage venture capital: Company now has a viable product that is ready for alpha testing with potential end users. Early-stage financing is typically used to build out the commercial-scale manufacturing services (no longer being built in the owner's garage)
- Second or late-stage expansion venture capital: Company may be breaking even or making its first profits; commercial viability is established. Operating cash flows are not enough to sustain growth yet.
- Mezzanine stage: The last stage before the company goes public or is sold to a strategic buyer. The financing at this stage is to keep the company from running out of cash before it goes public. At this stage, the company has a proven track record.

Explain the compound option that is embedded in most venture capital investments

- Money invested in each stage of a venture can be seen as the purchase of a call option on investing in the next stage of the venture
- An option expiration date is the point in time at which either additional capital has to be invested or the project is abandoned or sold

Discuss the concept of the J-curve in the context of a startup company

- Like VC funds, start-up companies lose money in the early stages and generate profits later

21.4 Demonstrate knowledge of the risk and return characteristics of venture capital investments.

For example:

Describe the sources of return (risk premiums) to venture capital investments and compare them with sources of return (risk premiums) for publicly traded equities

- Business risk of a start-up company
- Liquidity risk
- Lack of diversification associated with a VC portfolio

Describe access and vintage year diversification as keys to successful venture capital investment

- Two important keys to successful VC investing are:
    - Access to top-tier managers
    - Achieve vintage-year diversification – invest in funds of different vintage years

Discuss persistence of performance in venture capital firms

- Superior performance in a VC fund is usually a predictor of superior performance of the next fund since the best VVC firms attract the best entrepreneurs, business plans and investment opportunities

Recognize inferences that can be drawn from comparing definable characteristics of venture capital investments with their historical stand-alone and portfolio performances

- VC's lost money between 2000-10 according to the Cambridge Associates VC index
- Diversification benefits exist

21.5 Demonstrate knowledge of leveraged buyout (LBO) transactions.

For example:

Recognize how LBO transactions are distinguished from traditional investments in public securities

- The LBO buys out control of the assets
- The LBO uses debt
- The LBO itself is not publicly traded

Describe the structure of LBO funds and the role of various entities involved in LBO transactions

- LBO funds are typically structured as limited partnerships
- Some LBO funds have advisory boards to advise the GPs on strategic or transactional issues

Describe and apply fees associated with investments in LBO funds

- 1.25-3% management fee plus a 20-30% incentive fee
- The LBO fund may charge fees for arranging the buyout or a divestiture fee

Describe agency relationships, their associated costs, and their role as a potential source of return to LBO transactions

- LBO firms replace a dispersed group of shareholders (as is the case of a public company) with a highly concentrated group of equity owners
- This allows the management of the buyout firm to focus on maximizing cash flows
- The management is also given a significant equity stake to align interests with shareholders

Describe general categories of LBO transactions and how they create value

- Efficiency buyouts: Often lead to a reduction in firm assets and revenue with the goal of eventually increasing firm profits
- Spurring entrepreneurship: An LBO can free an operating company chained to its parent company
- The overstuffed corporation: an LBO can be used to dismantle inefficient conglomerates
- Buy-and-build strategies: Involves combining several operating companies or divisions through additional buyouts
- Turnaround strategies: Targets underperforming companies with excessive leverage and poor management

Discuss the characteristics of portfolio companies of LBO funds

- In a majority of cases, the PE firm gets the private company to stream line its workforce, reduce expenses, and increase its balance sheet capacity for more leverage

Describe how LBOs potentially improve the management of the target company

- The use of leverage where interest payments are tax deductible
- Less scrutiny from public equity investors and regulators
- Freedom from distracted corporate parent
- Potential of company management to become substantial equity holders

Identify and discuss performance enhancements and risks that arise as a result of LBOs

- The use of debt enhances performance but increases LBO risk
- After the LBO, the management of the company improves operations, streamlines expenses and implements better asset utilization

Apply various methods to value LBO transactions

- The value of the unlevered firm can be calculated using the constant dividend growth formula
- The IRR can be calculated using the CAGR formula with the above value as the ending value and the equity capital invested as the beginning value

Describe typical exit strategies of LBOs

- Sale to strategic buyer – most common
- IPO
- Refinance the debt via another LBO deal to compensate managers (leveraged recapitalization)
- Straight refinancing – company takes on debt to pay a dividend

- Buyout-to-buyout deal – sell the portfolio company to another buyout firm

Describe the concept of spillover of corporate governance to the public markets (the principles of corporate governance that LBOs apply to their private companies have four important benefits for the public market)

- The strong governance implemented should still be in place when the company is taken public again
- LBO deals are a warning to ineffective management of other public companies
- The incentive and monitoring schemes implemented by LBO firms for their portfolio companies provide guidance to managers and shareholders of other firms searching for more efficient methods
- As LBOs often target conglomerates, they can help stop unnecessary and inefficient diversification of conglomerates

Explain auction markets and club deals as alternatives to the single-sourced approach to funding LBO transactions

- An auction process often results in less upside for the LBO firm but reflects the maturation of the industry
- With club deals, LBO firms can contribute capital to the same deal and save costs to acquire a target and on due diligence

21.6 Demonstrate knowledge of the risk and return characteristics of LBOs.

For example:

Discuss the reasons why LBO funds have less risk than venture capital funds

- Buyouts target successful but undervalued companies with a long-term operating history
- LBO firms tend to be less specialized than VC firms and thus more diversified in their choice of targets
- An exit strategy of an IPO is more likely for an LBO deal (prior history as a public company) than a VC deal

Chapter 22: Debt Types of Private Equity

Keywords

Absolute priority: A rule that stipulates the order of payment - creditors before shareholders - in the event of liquidation.

Acceleration: A requirement that debt be repaid sooner than originally scheduled and typically forces default.

Assignment: When senior lenders typically restrict the rights of the mezzanine investor to assign (or sell) its interests to a third party.

Blanket subordination: Prevents any payment of principal or interest to the mezzanine investor until after the senior debt has been fully repaid.

Blocking position: A single creditor can block a plan of reorganization if it holds a third of the dollar amount of any class of claimants.

Chapter 11 bankruptcy: Chapter of the United States Bankruptcy Code, which permits reorganization under the bankruptcy laws of the United States.

Chapter 7 bankruptcy: Governs the process of a liquidation bankruptcy.

Classification of claims: When under a reorganization plan different classes of equity and bondholders are entitled to certain claims on the company's assets.

Cramdown: Involuntary imposition by a court of a reorganization plan over the objection of some classes of creditors.

Debtor-in-possession financing: Special form of financing provided for companies in financial distress or under Chapter 11 bankruptcy process. Usually, this debt is considered senior to all other debt, equity, and any other securities issued by a company. It gives a troubled company a new start, albeit under strict conditions.

Fulcrum securities: The junior securities most likely to convert to (or receive) equity in a reorganized company after it emerges from Chapter 11 of the Bankruptcy Code. Some investors purchase this security as part of a strategy to take ownership of the company. While in the past, the fulcrum security was unsecured debt, today it is increasingly secured debt. For example, lenders may provide DIP financing as part of a loan-to-own strategy, based on an analysis that the debt represented by the DIP financing may ultimately result in a controlling ownership position in the company.

Intercreditor agreement: Agreement among creditors that sets forth the various lien positions and the rights and liabilities of each creditor and its impact on the other creditors.

Loan-to-EBITDA multiple: Debt divided by EBITDA. Bank loans and senior loans usually require a multiple of no more than 2 to 2.5.

Mezzanine funds: Funds that provide mezzanine financing.

PIK toggle: With a PIK toggle note, the borrower in each interest period has the option to pay interest in cash or to PIK (let the interest payment accrue to the principal balance) the interest payment.

Plan of reorganization: A business plan for emerging from bankruptcy protection as a viable concern.

Prepackaged bankruptcy filing: When a debtor company agrees in advance (before filing Chapter 11) with its creditors on a plan of organization.

Springing subordination: Allows the mezzanine investor to receive interest payments while the senior debt is still outstanding. But if a default occurs or a covenant is violated, the subordination springs to stop all payments to the mezzanine investor until the default is cured or the senior debt has been fully repaid.

Stretch financing: Stretch loans are extended to those individuals or companies that are in dire need of financing.

Takeout provision: Allows the mezzanine investor to purchase the senior debt once it has been repaid to a specified level. Allows the mezzanine investor to become the most senior lender to the company and take control of the firm. At this point, the investor usually converts the debt into equity and becomes the largest shareholder of the company.

Weighted average cost of capital: Rate that a company is expected to pay on average to all its security holders to finance its assets.

Learning Objectives

22.1 Demonstrate knowledge of mezzanine debt.

For example:

Describe characteristics of mezzanine debt

- Appropriate for companies with reliable cash flow
- A much more passive investment than an LBO
- Higher risk profile than senior debt because of its unsecured status, lower credit priority and equity kicker

Describe the typical exit strategy for mezzanine debt investors

- When the underlying company goes public or obtains capital through a large equity issuance by the underlying company
- The mezzanine debt may also be paid prior to maturity if the borrowing firm is acquired or recapitalized; the mezzanine firm is repaid face value plus the sale of stock from the conversion rights or sale of warrants attached to the mezzanine debt

Analyze how mezzanine debt affects company cost of capital

- When mezzanine capital is added to the capital structure, WACC goes down

Apply weighted average cost of capital valuation to capital structures with mezzanine debt

- The WACC formula can be used, adding a term to represent the cost of mezzanine financing

Compare and contrast mezzanine debt to leveraged loans and high-yield bonds

- Mezzanine financing is typically used by middle market companies which typically do not have access to the large public debt markets
- Mezzanine financing is highly tailored to fit the borrower which makes it very illiquid; an exit involves a lengthy negotiation process
- Mezzanine financing carries a higher coupon than senior debt as it is not backed by collateral (commonality with high yield)
- Leveraged loans typically do not have an equity kicker, have the strictest debt covenants and a first lien on assets

Describe seven typical examples of transactions that use mezzanine debt

- MBOs
- Financing for growth and expansion
- Acquisitions
- Recapitalizations
- Commercial real estate
- LBOs

- Bridge financing

Describe types of mezzanine debt investors and recognize their motivations

- Mezzanine funds: Investors are typically institutions. Typically structured and charge fees similar to hedge funds and traditional private equity funds
- Insurance companies: Major source of mezzanine financing because the duration of their liabilities are best matched with longer-term debt instruments
- Traditional senior lenders
- Traditional VC firms

Identify and describe eight characteristics that distinguish mezzanine debt from other types of financing

- Board representation sometimes with full voting rights
- Restrictions on the borrower RE additional debt, acquisitions, etc.
- Flexibility of terms
- Negotiations with senior creditors via an intercreditor agreement
- Subordination which may either be a blanket subordination or a springing subordination
- The violation of any covenant may result in acceleration
- Senior lenders typically restrict the mezzanine investor from assigning interests in the loan to a third party
- Takeout provisions: The heart of mezzanine investing and one of the most important provisions in the intercreditor agreement

22.2 Demonstrate knowledge of distressed debt as a form of private equity investment.

For example:

Recognize characteristics of distressed debt

- Debt that has deteriorated in quality since issuance
- Within the risk spectrum, private equity distressed debt investors fall between LBO firms and venture capital

Describe the supply of distressed debt

- LBO firms are a great source of distressed debt since sometimes the debt burden becomes too much to bear (leveraged fallouts)

Describe the demand for distressed debt

- Distressed debt is attractive to vulture investors due to its inefficient market
- Can be used by investors as a way to gain an equity stake in the company

Explain typical distressed debt investment strategies

- An active approach with intent to gain control of the company sometimes via fulcrum securities

- An investor that wants to have a hand in the reorganization and bankruptcy process short of taking control of the company
- Passive or opportunistic investment

Describe two major types of corporate bankruptcy processes

- Chapter 7: Liquidation
- Chapter 11: Reorganization

Identify the various terms and standards that relate to bankruptcy processes

- Classification of claims
- Prepackaged bankruptcy filing
- Blocking position
- Cramdown
- Absolute priority

22.3 Demonstrate knowledge of the risks associated with investments in distressed debt.

For example:

Discuss the role of business risk in distressed debt investing

- Business risk is the main risk in distressed debt investing
- A troubled company may ultimately prove to be worthless and unable to pay off its creditors

Chapter 23: Credit Risk and the Structuring of Cash Flows

Keywords

Arbitrage-free model: A financial engineering model that assigns prices to derivatives or other instruments in such a way that it is impossible to construct arbitrages between two or more of those prices. For example, if an option pricing formula assigned prices to put and call options that violated put-call parity, that would not be an arbitrage-free model.

Black-Scholes option pricing model: Method used to price options given the following assumptions:

- The price of the underlying asset follows a lognormal distribution.
- The (continuous) risk-free rate is constant and known.
- The volatility of the underlying asset is constant and known.
- Markets are "frictionless."
- The underlying asset generates no cash flows.
- The options are European.

Bull option spreads: Can be formed with calls (combination of a long w/ $70 strike price and short call w/ $90 strike price) or puts (combination of a long w/ $70 strike price and short put w/ $90 strike price). Betting that the price of the asset will increase but caps upside.

Calibrate a model: To establish values for the key parameters in a model, such as default probability or an asset volatility.

Collateralized debt obligation (CDO): A CDO is an Asset Backed Security that is collateralized by a pool of debt obligations. A CDO has the following structure: one or more senior tranches, several levels of mezzanine tranches, and a subordinate (equity) tranche to provide prepayment and credit protection.

Credit risk: Risk associated with the failure of a company or counterparty to fulfill its obligation.

Credit spread risk: Spread risk is the possibility that a bond loses value because its credit spread widens relative to its benchmark.

Default risk: Probability of default of a debt issuer.

Detachment point: In case of a tranche of a CDO, the point beyond which losses do not affect the tranche in question.

Downgrade risk: The risk that the creditworthiness of a borrower has changed.

Equity tranche: Tranche with residual claim to the cash flows of the underlying assets.

Lower attachment point: The first percentage loss in the collateral pool that begins to cause reduction in a tranche.

Merton's structural model: Model that equates owning risky to owning riskless debt and writing a put option that allows the stockholders to put the assets of the firm to the debt holder without further liability.

Mezzanine tranche: CDO tranche between senior and equity.

Put-call parity: Put-call parity for European options says that the cost of a fiduciary call (long call, long bond) must be equal to the cost of a protective put (long put, long underlying asset). Put-call parity can be used to demonstrate how to create synthetic instruments. For example, a synthetic call is a long put, a long stock position, and a short position in a pure-discount risk-free bond. Investors create these synthetic securities to exploit relative mispricing among the four securities.

Long Call + Riskless bond = Long Put + Underlying Asset

Ratings migration: A positive or negative change in a credit rating.

Recovery rate: Amount recovered through foreclosure or bankruptcy procedures in event of a default, expressed as a percentage of face value.

Reduced-form models: Models that do not attempt to look at the structural reasons for the default event but take rating changes as events that take place with a particular probability and attempt to model this probability and insert the probability into a pricing equation.

Risk-neutral probabilities: Statistical probabilities that if used would correctly give the fair price of a security under the assumption that investors are risk-neutral.

Senior tranche: Tranche with higher claim to the cash flows of the underlying assets.

Structural models: Models that take into account various underlying factors that drive the default process.

Structuring of cash flows: Process of dividing a stream of cash into two or more streams that differ with regard to timing.

Tranche: A security issued to finance a portfolio with specified claims to the cash flows from the portfolio.

Upper attachment point: Same as detachment point. The higher percentage loss point at which the given tranche is completely wiped out.

Learning Objectives

23.1 Demonstrate knowledge of credit risk.

For example:

Explain default risk

- The risk that a bond issuer or the debtor on a loan will not repay the interest and principal payments on the outstanding debt in full

Explain downgrade risk

- The risk that the creditworthiness of a borrower has changed as indicated by a rating agency's change t the borrower's credit rating
- Ratings migration

Explain credit spread risk

- The risk that the credit spread will change as a result of changes in overall market conditions (or macro events) and/or the creditworthiness of the particular borrower
- In an economic contraction, revenues and earnings decline across industries, reducing interest coverage for loans and bonds

23.2 Demonstrate knowledge of approaches to credit risk modeling.

For example:

Distinguish structural and reduced-form credit risk models

- Structural: Takes into account the underlying assets and the structuring of the cash flows of a particular issue
- Reduced form: Uses analysis and observations of similar credit risks over time to understand a particular credit issue

Explain arbitrage-free credit risk models

- Can generate prices that are consistent with current observed prices of the most liquid segments of the credit market

23.3 Demonstrate knowledge of the structural approach to credit risk modeling.

For example:

Recognize the option-like nature of structured cash flows

- The equity in a leveraged corporation is like a call option on the assets of a firm, with a strike price equal to the face value of the debt

- If the firm does well, it pays its debt holders fully when the debt matures and the assets of the firm belong to the equity shareholders
- If the firm does poorly, the shareholders of the firm can declare bankruptcy and walk away from the firm, leaving the assets to the debt holders
- Option-based view of the firm's debt
  - Owning debt is equivalent to owning the assets and writing a call option
  - Owning debt is equivalent to owning a covered call – being long the assets and short a call option on those assets

Recognize the intuition of Merton's structural model

- Applies to credit risk modeling
- Put-call parity can show the option-like nature of owning risky debt

Owning credit risky debt is equivalent to the following options positions:
Covered call   =   Owning riskless debt and writing a put option on firm assets
Assets – call   =   Riskless bond – Put
This side of the equation is more commonly used within the structural model to illustrate the put option-like aspects of owning risky debt; the put option is the ability of the equity owners to declare bankruptcy and enjoy limited liability

Recognize and apply the mechanics of Merton's structural model

- Assumes that bond default can only take place at its maturity
- Value of the firm [V(t)] = market value of equity [S(t)] + current value of debt [B(t,T)]
- Payoff to bondholders = Bond principal value (K) – max(K – Firm Value at time T, 0)
- Payoff to shareholders = max(0, Firm Value at time T – K)
- At maturity, bondholders receive K (principal + interest) unless the firm assets are worth less than that; in that instance, the bondholders will take over the firm and receive the value of the firm's assets
- When the debt matures, shareholders will receive the residual value if the firm's asset value exceeds the debt's notional value

Recognize and apply the binomial option approach to pricing structured cash flows

- Used to value the put option component of a risky bond
- Two points in time: today and one period from today
- Only two possible outcomes to the value of the firm's assets
- Shows the pricing and credit spread of risky debt as a function of the price of the put option, which in turn depends on the value and the riskiness of the firm's assets
- Using the risk neutral pricing approach, the value of a put is:
  - $V(0) = \frac{1}{1+r} [\pi * V_u + (1 - \pi)*V_d]$
  - π = risk-neutral probability of an up movement
  - $1- \pi$ = risk-neutral probability of a down movement

- o r = riskless one-period rate
- Application
  - o First solve for π with V(0) being the value of the firm's assets
  - o Then sub values into the formula and solve for the value of the put
  - o Value of the risky bond = B(0,1) = PV of riskless bond – put value = $\frac{K}{1+r}$ – P(0)
- Can use the above values to calculate credit spread (s)
  - o $B(0,1) = \frac{Bond\ face\ value}{1+r+s}$
  - o Solve for s which translates to the yield of the risky bond minus the yield of the risk-free bond

Recognize the Black-Scholes approach to pricing structured cash flows

- Assumes continuous-time trading and allows an infinite number of outcomes by assuming that asset returns are lognormally distributed
- More realistic portrayal of asset prices
- Expressed as the price of a European put option on the firm's assets depending on five variables:
  - o Value of the firm
  - o Notional value of the bond (principal + interest that bondholders will receive if the firm doesn't default)
  - o Risk-free rate
  - o Time to maturity
  - o Volatility of the rate of return on the firm's assets (standard deviation)

Discuss advantages and disadvantages of structural credit risk models

- Advantages
  - o Relies on data from equity markets, which is generally seen as more reliable than bond markets
  - o This also allows bond instruments to be priced independently rather than from suing credit spread information from related bond instruments
  - o Structural models are oriented towards the fundamentals of the specific company
- Disadvantages
  - o Equity markets may provide poor indications of how credit markets should be priced if equity prices are irrationally inflated
  - o Generally inappropriate for sovereign issuers

23.4 Demonstrate knowledge of the reduced-form approach to credit risk modeling.

For example:

Recognize and apply the concept of expected loss due to credit risk

- Expected credit loss = PD * EAD * (1 – R)
  - o PD = probability of default

- EAD = exposure at default or the nominal value of the position that is exposed to default at the time of default (e.g., amount lent * 1+interest rate)
- LGD = loss given default or the economic loss in case of default = 1-R
- R = recovery rate – percentage of credit exposure that the lender ultimately receives through the bankruptcy process

Recognize and apply the risk-neutral approach to pricing risky bonds

- Assumes that investors require the same rate of return on investments regardless of levels and types of risk because investors are indifferent with regard to how much risk they bear
- Assumes risk neutrality – that investors don't require a premium for bearing risk
- A risky one-period zero coupon with face value of K can be valued as:
  - $\frac{K}{1+r} * [R*\lambda + (1-\lambda)]$
  - R = expected recovery rate in case of default
  - λ = probability of default; used to weight the probability of two outcomes – default and no default

Recognize and apply credit spreads within the reduced-form approach

- First calculate the probability of default:
  - $\lambda = \frac{1}{1-R} * (\frac{s}{1+r+s})$
  - s = use credit spreads on comparable bonds; in a problem, you may be given the risk-free rate (e.g, 5%) and the typical bond yield (e.g,. 6%) and so the implied spread (s) used would be 1% (6%-5%)
- Then plug into this formula to calculate the bond credit spread:
  - $s \approx \lambda * (1-R)$

Discuss how the relationships from risk-neutral models can be generalized

- Risky bonds with zero beta have true default probabilities equal to the risk-neutral default probability and offer an expected return equal to the riskless rate
- High-beta bonds have true default probabilities less than the risk-neutral default probability and an expected return higher than the riskless rate
- By using risk-neutral probabilities as if they were true default probabilities, the true prices of bonds can be calculated regardless of whether their risks are entirely idiosyncratic or partially systematic

Discuss the application of the reduced-form approach to valuing different bonds within the same capital structure (that differ in seniority – e.g., junior and senior debt)

- The reduced-form approach often focuses on relative pricing using information from more liquid segments of the market
- The reduced-form approach relates credit spreads to recovery rates – senior debt is expected to have a higher recovery rate than junior debt

- Can use the credit spread and recovery rate of one class of debt to calculate the probability of default and credit spread for another class of debt

Discuss advantages and disadvantages of reduced-form credit risk models

- Advantages
  - Ability to calculate the models using derivatives
  - Models are extremely tractable and are well-suited for pricing derivatives and portfolio products
- Disadvantages
  - Sensitive to assumptions, particularly the recovery rate
  - There may be limited information about the bonds that are needed to calibrate the model
  - Long-term recovery rates may not accurately predict future recovery rates if the economic fundamentals have shifted

23.5 Demonstrate knowledge of the concept of structuring cash flows using collateralized debt obligations (CDO).

For example:

Explain the concept of a CDO using a stylized example

- Structures cash flows from multiple debt securities into multiple claims (tranches)
- After fees and expenses, CDO cash flows are distributed to the various tranches in order of their seniority
- The equity tranches have residual claims

Discuss attachment points and detachment points

- Attachment points
  - The first percentage loss in the collateral pool that begins to cause reduction in a tranche
  - Lower attachment point
- Detachment points
  - Upper attachment point
  - The higher percentage loss point at which the given tranche is completely wiped out

Explain the relationship between option spreads, mezzanine tranches, and other tranches

- The structural model view of mezzanine debt is that it contains a bull option spread that can be formed with calls or puts

Chapter 24: Credit Derivatives

Keywords

American credit options: May be exercised at any time before the expiration date.

Binary options: Type of option where the payoff is either some fixed amount of some asset or nothing at all.

CDS indices: Portfolios of single-name default swaps. They are tradable products that allow investors to create long or short positions in baskets of credits.

Counterparty risk: The risk to each party of a contract that the counterparty will not live up to its contractual obligations.

Credit default swap: In a credit default swap (CDS), one party pays a quarterly percentage of the face value of a debt security. If a credit event occurs, the other party pays the difference between the face value of the debt and its value after a credit event (cash settlement) or pays face value in return for delivery of the bonds (physical settlement).

Credit derivatives: Refers to any one of "various instruments and techniques designed to separate and then transfer the credit risk" of the underlying loan. It is a securitized derivative whereby the credit risk is transferred to an entity other than the lender.

Credit protection buyer: The buyer of the CDS makes a series of payments (the CDS "fee" or "spread") to the seller and, in exchange, receives a payoff if the loan defaults.

Credit protection seller: Pays the credit protection buyer after a credit event.

Credit-linked notes (CLNs): A security with an embedded credit default swap allowing the issuer to transfer a specific credit risk to credit investors. Under this structure, the coupon or price of the note is linked to the performance of a reference asset. It offers borrowers a hedge against credit risk, and gives investors a higher yield on the note for accepting exposure to a specified credit event.

Derivatives: Financial instrument which derives its value from the value of underlying entities such as an asset, index, or interest rate.

European credit options: May be exercised only at the expiration date of the option.

Funded credit derivatives: Involves the protection seller (the party that assumes the credit risk) making an initial payment that is used to settle any potential credit events. The protection buyer, however, still may be exposed to the credit risk of the protection seller itself (counterparty risk).

Mark-to-market adjustment: Process of changing the value of a CDS in the accounting and financial systems of the CDS parties.

Multi-name instruments: Allow investors and issuers to transfer some or all of the credit risk associated with a portfolio of defaultable securities.

Novation: In a safe trading environment, the parties to a trade need to be assured that their counterparty will honor the trade, no matter how the market has moved. To ensure this, a clearing house interposes themselves as counterparties to every trade and extends a guarantee that the trade will be settled as originally intended.

Operational risk in derivatives:

Referenced asset: The underlying asset for the derivative (CDS) that affects the subsequent payments under the contract.

Single-name credit derivatives: The simplest - and most common - type of credit default swap is one where there is just one reference entity or borrower.

Standard ISDA agreement: Standardized terms for CDS.

Total return swap: In a total return swap, the total return on a debt security (interest plus the change in bond value) is paid by one party to another party, who pays either a fixed or floating rate of interest in return.

Unfunded credit derivatives: Bilateral contract between two counterparties, where each party is responsible for making its payments under the contract (i.e. payments of premiums and any cash or physical settlement amount).

Learning Objectives

24.1 Demonstrate knowledge of credit derivative markets.

For example:

Explain how a bank can use credit derivatives to transfer credit risk

- A bank can still make large loans to a client, retain the relationship but transfer the risk via credit derivatives and still have a diversified balance sheet
- However, this process increases counterparty risk to the banks that they buy credit derivatives from

Recognize three groupings of credit derivatives: single-name versus multi-name, funded versus unfunded, and sovereign versus non-sovereign

- Single-name versus multi-name
    - Single name: Most common type of credit derivative; most are CDS;
    - Multi-name: Credit indices are an example
- Funded (require cash outlays) versus unfunded (exchange of payments does not occur until a default occurs)
- Sovereign (additional political and macro risk) versus non-sovereign (e.g., corporate)

Describe the four stages of credit derivative activity

- 1. Defensive stage: late 1980s to early 1990s and characterized by ad hoc attempts by banks to lay off some of their credit exposures
- 2. 1991-mid/late 1990s: Emergence of intermediated market and investors enter the market to seek exposure to credit risk; e.g., total return swap
- 3. 1999-2003; Maturing from a new product to one resembling other forms of derivatives; dealers began warehousing risks and running hedged and diversified portfolios of credit derivatives
- 4. 2003-present; The development of a liquid market and standardized practices (e.g., standard settlement dates)

24.2 Demonstrate knowledge of credit default swaps.

For example:

Compare and contrast credit default swaps and total return swaps

- Credit default swaps
    - Credit protection buyer pays a periodic premium in exchange for a contingent payment
    - The protection buyer may have a cash position in the credit-risky asset and is using a CDS to buy credit protection
- Total return swaps
    - The owner of the credit-risky asset pays the total return of the asset to the credit protection seller and receives a certain payment

- o The credit protection buyer gives up the uncertain amounts of the credit-risky asset in return for certain payments
- o The credit protection seller receives both the upside and downside of the return associated with the credit-risky asset

Explain the mechanics of credit default swaps including standard provisions and parameters

- Standard provisions per the ISDA
  - o CDS spread: Premium paid by the credit protection buyer is called the spread. Quoted in basis points per annum on the notion al value of the CDS.
  - o Contract size: No imposed size limits or length of term
  - o Trigger events: Six kinds of potential trigger events that will determine when the credit protection seller must make a payment to the buyer:
    - Bankruptcy
    - Failure to pay – company is unable to meet debt obligations (pre-bankruptcy)
    - Restructuring that is disadvantageous to the holder of the referenced credit
    - Obligation acceleration (due to covenant)
    - Obligation default
    - Repudiation/moratorium – Refusal by a sovereign government to pay its debt
  - o Settlement: Can be done by cash or physical settlement (credit protection seller buys the debt at par value; more common)
  - o Delivery: The credit protection buyer has a choice of assets that can be delivered for physical settlement
- Four parameters that define a CDS
  - o Credit reference: The referenced bond or obligation
  - o Notional amount: The amount of credit risk being transferred
  - o CDS spread: The annual payment for credit protection
  - o CDS maturity: CDS contracts expire on the 20th of March, June, September or December

Explain the marking to market of credit default swaps

- CDS contracts have zero market values to each side at inception
- Mark to market adjustments are made for financial reporting, realizing economic gains & losses and for managing collateral
- Calculating a CDS MTM adjustment is about the same as calculating the cost of entering into an offsetting transaction

Explain three methods for unwinding credit default swap transactions

- Enter an offsetting position
- Assign the contract to another party with the original counterparty's permission
- Terminate the contract with mutual consent by paying the other counterparty any lost value from discontinuing the swap

Recognize typical credit default swap market participants and their swap transactions

- Major banks – market makers
- Bank loan portfolios – banks use the CDS market to hedge exposure
- Hedge funds: Use CDS market to buy and sell credit risk
- Other asset managers: The CDS market offers opportunities that they cannot find in the bond market
- Insurance companies: Sell credit protection
- Corporations: Use the CDS markets to manage credit exposure to third parties

Identify and explain five typical motivations for using credit default swaps

- Efficient way to decompose and separate risks embedded in complex securities independent of interest rate risks
- Efficient way to hedge credit risk by shorting credit and establish synthetic short positions
- Can synthetically create loan or bond substitutes through tailor-made credit products
- The high liquidity of credit derivatives can be a source of information that links structurally separate markets. CDS spread changes may occur before the pricing is reflected in less liquid markets.
- Provide liquidity during times of turbulence in the credit markets when it may be hard to sell bonds even at reduced prices. Investors can reduce long credit risk by buying credit protection

24.3 Demonstrate knowledge of credit options and credit-linked notes.

For example:

Contrast credit default swaps and credit options

- Credit default swaps
    - Not considered options as they do not offer the buyer the right but not an obligation to enter a transaction and do not usually require just a single upfront premium
    - But are option-like in that they offer an asymmetric payout stream
    - Payments are triggered by specific events and are not subject to the discretion of the parties as in options
- Credit options
    - Involve a single payment from the credit protection buyer to the seller that leads to an asymmetric payout
    - The decision to exercise may be made by the option buyer or may be automatically generated by trigger events depending on the terms

Recognize the terminology of credit options

- Credit call (put) option – allows holder to buy (sell) a credit-risky price or rate
- Since prices and spreads move inversely, a call option on a price is the opposite bet as a call option on a rate
- Binary options
- American vs. European options

Explain call options on credit default swaps

- A call option on a CDS allows the holder to enter a CDS at the rate (strike) specified in the option contract
- If the credit spread widens, the call option holder may choose to enter a CDS at the prespecified spread by exercising the option
- With a call option, if the credit improves it just expires out of the money
- With a CDS, the investor doesn't benefit if the credit improves

Describe credit-linked notes

- Bonds issued with an embedded credit option
- Can be issued with reference to the credit risk of a single corporation or to a basket of credit risks
- If there is a default, downgrade, or other adverse credit event, the holder of the note receives a lower coupon and/or only a partial redemption of the principal value
- The holder has essentially sold credit protection to the issuer
- In the event of no default, the holder receives a higher yield (risk-free yield + premium)

24.4 Demonstrate knowledge of the risks of credit derivatives.

For example:

Explain excessive credit exposure using off-balance-sheet derivatives, pricing risk from over-the-counter derivatives, and liquidity risk of over-the-counter derivatives

- There's the risk that traders or portfolio managers may use CDS to obtain excessive and imprudent leverage; because they are off-balance sheet contracts excessive credit exposure can be achieved without appearing on an investor's balance sheet
- Valuation subjectivity and discretion in the assumptions made can also result in pricing risk
- Credit derivatives are also illiquid and a party may not be able to get fair value upon exiting the position. Also, they cannot be sold without the other party's permission

Explain the counterparty risk of over-the-counter credit default swaps and the basis risk of credit default swaps

- Counterparty risk
  - In the case of an OTC option, only the long position is exposed to counterparty risk
  - With a CDS, the primary counterparty risk is held by the protection buyer
- Basis risk
  - Risk due to imperfect correlation between the values of the CDS and the asset being hedged by the protection buyer
  - The reference entity specified in the CDS may not precisely match the asset being hedged
  - May be done because hedging the asset exactly results in more customization and ultimately less liquidity for the CDS

Describe credit default swap index products

- CDS indices are portfolios of single-name default swaps
- They are tradable products that allow investors to create long or short positions in baskets of credits
- CDX – North American and emerging markets
- iTraxx – Europe and Asia
- Indices roll every six months and the market is very liquid (smaller liquidity premium than single-name CDS

Chapter 25: Collateralized Debt Obligations

Keywords

Amortization period: Last part of the CDO life cycle during which the manager of the CDO stops reinvesting excess cash flows and begins to wind down the CDO by repaying the CDO debt securities.

Arbitrage CDOs: A CDO in which the arranger sets out to acquire exposures to take advantage of the difference between spreads on the underlying portfolio and spreads on the CDO liabilities.

Balance sheet CDOs: CDOs can be balance sheet-driven, in which the motivation is to remove assets (and the associated funding) from the balance sheet.

Bankruptcy remote: When insolvency of the bankruptcy remote entity has as little economic impact as possible on other entities within the group. A bankruptcy remote entity is often a single-purpose entity. If the sponsoring bank or money manager goes bankrupt, the CDO trust is not affected.

Cash flow CDO: In a cash flow CDO, the portfolio manager seeks to generate sufficient cash flow (from interest and principal payments) to repay the senior and mezzanine tranches.

Cash-funded CDO: Involves the actual purchase of the portfolio of securities serving as the collateral for the trust and to be held in the trust.

Collateralized fund obligation (CFO): Form of securitization involving private equity fund or hedge fund assets, similar to collateralized debt obligations. CFOs are a structured form of financing for diversified private equity portfolios, layering several tranches of debt ahead of the equity holders.

Copula approach: Approach to analyzing the credit risk of a CDO that may be viewed like a simulation of possible default rates and their implication on the cash flows to various tranches.

Distressed debt CDOs: CDOs that use the CDO structure to securitize and structure the risks and returns of a portfolio of distressed debt securities, where the primary collateral is distressed debt.

Diversity score: A numerical estimation of the extent to which a portfolio is diversified.

External credit enhancement: External credit enhancements are financial guarantees from a third party that are used to supplement other forms of credit enhancements. The third-party guarantee effectively links the ABS to the credit risk of the third-party guarantor. Third-party guarantees include: corporate guarantee, letter of credit, and bond insurance.

Financial engineering risk: Potential loss attributable to securitization, structuring of cash flows, options, and other applications of innovative financing devices.

Internal credit enhancement: Internal credit enhancements are "internal" to the issue—they do not rely on a third-party guarantee. Internal credit enhancements include reserve funds, overcollateralization, and senior/subordinated structure.

Market value CDO: The underlying portfolio is actively traded without a focus on cash flow matching of assets and liabilities.

Overcollateralization: The process of posting more collateral than is needed to obtain or secure financing. It is a form of credit enhancement.

Ramp-up period: First part of the CDO life cycle during which the CDO trust issues securities (tranches) and uses the proceeds from the CDO note sale to acquire the initial collateral pool (the assets).

Reference portfolio: The underlying portfolio or pool of assets held in the SPV within the CDO structure.

Reserve account: Holds excess cash in highly rated instruments such as Treasuries or high-grade commercial paper to provide security to the debt holders of the CLO trust.

Revolving period: Second phase of the CDO life cycle during which the manager of the CDO trust may actively manage the collateral pool for the CDO, potentially buying and selling securities and reinvesting the excess cash flows received from the CDO collateral pool.

Risk shifting: The process of altering the risk of an asset or a portfolio in a manner that disproportionately affects the risks and values of related securities and the investors that own those securities.

Single-tranche CDOs: A CDO that may have multiple tranches but the sponsor issues (sells) only one tranche from the capital structure and keeps the rest on its balance sheet.

Special purpose vehicle (SPV): Special corporation or trust to established to buy the assets that are securitized, issue the securities and keep it off the parent balance sheet. Advantageous for investors because their interests are better protected in an SPV than on the BS of an intermediary if it were to go bankrupt.

Sponsor of the trust: Establishes the trust and bears the associated administrative and legal costs.

Spread compression risk: Risk of when credit spreads decline or compress over time, reducing interest rate receipts from the CDO's collateral.

Subordination: The most common form of credit enhancement in a CDO transaction and is the process of protecting a given security by issuing other securities that have a lower seniority to cash flows.

Synthetic CDO: When the CDO does not actually own the underlying assets.

Weighted average rating factor (WARF): Measures the risk of the underlying collateral pool and its diversity score.

Weighted average spread (WAS): Spread over LIBOR used as a measure of return.

Yield curve risk: Risk of changes in the yield curve as represented by shifts in its level, its slope and its shape.

Learning Objectives

25.1 Demonstrate knowledge of collateralized debt obligations (CDOs).

For example:

Describe the history of CDOs

- CDO structures began in the late 1980s
- One of the first major uses was for high yield bonds
- Originally these deals focused on bonds and were called CBOs

Describe the general structure and life cycle of a CDO

- Stage 1: Ramp-up period – when the CDO trust issues securities and uses the proceeds to acquire the assets
- Stage 2: Revolving period – Active management phase (buying, selling, reinvesting excess cash flows)
- Stage 3: Amortization period – Winding down the CDO by repaying the CDO debt securities

Explain the terminology and details of CDOs

- Reference portfolio, WARF, WAS, diversity score

25.2 Demonstrate knowledge of balance sheet CDOs and arbitrage CDOs.

For example:

Discuss the purposes and attributes of balance sheet CDOs

- Banks use balance sheet CDOs to manage the assets on their balance sheets – reduce credit exposure, raise capital, meet regulatory capital requirements
- The CDO's asset manager is usually the selling bank which manages the portfolio of loans that it sold to the CDO trust via the SPV

Discuss the purposes and attributes of arbitrage CDOs

- Primarily motivated by a goal of successful selection and management of the CDO assets
- Designed to make a profit by capturing a spread for the equity investors in the CDO (the difference between the higher-yielding securities inside the CDO and the lower yield paid out to the tranches) and from fees

Describe and apply a typical arbitrage CDO structure

- Each tranche has its own credit rating
- The senior tranches have the highest priority against the trust collateral with lower coupon, yield and volatility
- The mezzanine tranche is below the senior tranche but above the equity tranche

- Equity tranche – bears the first losses

Analyze the cash flows in a typical arbitrage CDO structure

- The first priority for the cash flows from the collateral pool pays trust fees and expenses (e.g., management fees)
- Then, cash flows go to tranches in order to seniority
- The equity tranche is the first to suffer losses – default losses lower the value of the collateral assets and the flow of coupon income

25.3 Demonstrate knowledge of cash-funded CDOs and synthetic CDOs.

For example:

Compare and contrast cash-funded CDOs and synthetic CDOs

- Cash-funded CDOs – physical ownership of the assets in acquired in the CDO
- Synthetic CDOs – the CDO does not actually own the underlying assets

Explain how a cash-funded CDO can be used to reduce required regulatory capital

- Cash CDOs enable banks to replace risky assets on the balance sheet with cash

Apply a typical cash-funded CDO structure

- Sometimes the equity tranche of a CDO is unappealing to potential investors and the bank may have to retain an equity position in the trust
- Regulatory capital standards require that the bank risk-based capital equal to its first loss position

Describe the characteristics of synthetic CDOs

- Gains credit exposure through the use of total return swaps or credit default swaps
- The CDO trust sells credit protection on a references basket of assets
- For this protection, the CDO receives income (CDS payments) from the credit protection buyer
- Total return that would be earned from physical ownership is replicated from the sum of the CDS payments and interest from collateral received from issuing tranches

25.4 Demonstrate knowledge of cash flow and market value CDOs.

For example:

Describe the characteristics of cash flow CDOs

- Typically a fixed maturity for CDO liabilities that coincides with the maturity of the underlying CDO portfolio assets
- The CDO manager should focus on maintaining sufficient credit quality for the underlying portfolio such that the portfolio can redeem the liabilities issued by the CDO

Describe the characteristics of market value CDOs

- Underlying portfolio is actively traded without a focus on cash flow matching of assets and liabilities
- CDO liabilities are paid off through the trading and sale of the underlying portfolio

25.5 Demonstrate knowledge of credit risk and enhancement of CDOs.

For example:

Describe subordination as a CDO credit enhancement

- Internal credit enhancement
- Most common form of credit enhancement
- The process of protecting a security by issuing other securities with a lower seniority to cash flows

Describe excess spread as an internal CDO enhancement

- The average coupon on the assets > the average coupon paid on the tranches
- In this case, the CDO is able to receive more cash than it is required to pay out

Describe excess cash as an internal CDO enhancement

- Excess cash reserves in highly rated instruments (e.g., US Treasuries) are used to provide security to the debt holders of the trust
- Cash reserves are often used in the initial phase of a cash flow transaction
- Sometimes argues as not the most efficient form of credit enhancement since cash earns a lower rate of return than that required to fund the CDO securities

Describe external credit enhancements to CDOs

- Provided by an outside third party
- May be an insurance contract, the purchase of a put option by a CDO, or a CDS to protect against loan losses

Explain the effects of risk shifting on the tranches of CDOs

- Risk shifting is the process of altering the risk of an asset or a portfolio in a manner that disproportionately affects the risks and values of related securities and the investors that own those securities
- For example, increases in the risks of the CDO's assets transfers wealth from holders of the senior tranches to holders of less senior tranches

25.6 Demonstrate knowledge of new developments in CDOs.

For example:

Describe distressed debt CDOs

- Underlying CDO portfolio is made up of distressed debt
- CDOs usually made up of a combination of defaulted securities, distressed but unimpaired securities, and nondistressed securities
- Securities can receive a higher investment rating than the underlying distressed collateral through diversification, subordination or other credit enhancement tools
- The main suppliers of assets for distressed debt CDO have been banks

Describe hedge fund CDOs

- Collateralized fund obligations – applies CDO structure to hedge funds
- CDOs made up of hedge funds

Describe single-tranche CDOs

- A CDO that may have multiple tranches but the sponsor only issues one tranche from the capital structure
- The sponsor might sell one tranche and keep the rest on its balance sheet
- Allow for more customization for an investor

25.7 Demonstrate knowledge of the risks of CDOs.

For example:

Recognize the risks related to the underlying collateral

- Single greatest drier of risk associated with a CDO
- A CDO does not change the risk of the underlying assets; it merely distributes the risk to the various tranches
- Credit risk – credit spread risk, downgrade risk and default risk

Recognize the financial engineering risk

- Financial engineering may allocate risks in complex ways that aren't understood
- 1994 CMO crisis and 2007 mortgage crisis

Describe the CDO risk due to differences in the periodicity and payment dates of a CDO

- When payments are received on the underlying collateral may not be the same as when payments must be made on CDO securities (semiannual vs. quarterly payments)
- The problem is often solved with a swap agreement with an outside party where the CDO trust swaps payments on the underlying collateral in return for interest payments that match the trust securities

Explain the basis risk and spread compression risk

- Basis risk: When the index used to determine the interest earned on the CDO trust collateral is different from the index used to calculate the interest to be paid on the CDO securities; this will cause the cash flows to be different

- Spread compression risk: When credit spreads decline or compress over time, reducing interest rate receipts from the CDO's collateral

Describe the yield curve risk

- Risk of shifts in the yield curve (level, slope and shape)

Describe how CDO credit risk can be modeled

- Copula method is the primary method for determining the risks of tranches due to default risk
- Idea behind the model: Defaults are generated by two normally distributed factors: an idiosyncratic factor and a market factor

Topic 8: Risk Management and Portfolio Management

Chapter 26: Lessons from Hedge Fund Failures

Keywords

Affinity fraud: The commission of fraud against a group of people (or entities) that share something in common with the perpetrator (race, religion, etc.).

Anchoring: A tendency for an analyst to rely too heavily on previous beliefs.

Behavioral biases: Tendencies exhibited by humans that conflict with prescriptions based on rationality and empiricism.

Behavioral finance: A field of finance that proposes psychology-based theories to explain stock market anomalies.

Confirmation bias: Tendency of people to favor information that confirms their beliefs or hypotheses.

Leverage: Another word for debt.

Option collar: Option strategy that limits the range of possible positive or negative returns on an underlying to a specific range.

Ponzi scheme: Fraudulent investment operation that pays returns to its investors from their own money or the money paid by subsequent investors.

Restitution: Restoration of lost funds to investors, typically as a result of being victims of fraud.

Return on assets: Net income divided by total assets.

Return on equity: Net income divided by the book value of shareholders equity.

Window dressing: Legal and illegal strategies used to improve the outward appearance of an investment vehicle.

Learning Objectives

26.1 Demonstrate knowledge of the effect of market forces in generating hedge fund losses.

For example:

Discuss the collapse of Amaranth Advisors, LLC, the due diligence issues related to it, and lessons learned from the case

- Amaranth Advisors (est. 2000) was a multi-strategy hedge fund investing across asset classes and strategies
- But it made a very concentrated bet (50%) in the energy markets (natural gas) by 2006
- Risk mangers allowed the firm to take more risk than justified
- Lack of regulation in hedge fund and natural gas environments
- When VaR are estimated with historical data that reflect an abnormally calm period, they underestimate risk
- Liquidating large positions in illiquid markets can move markets against you causing further losses

Discuss the collapse of Peloton Partners, the due diligence issues related to it, and lessons learned from the case

- Peloton Partners (est. 2005) had a swift collapse
- Made a substantial bet in 2007 that the mortgage bond market would collapse
- It earned an 87% return as mortgage prices fell but incurred losses as the market continued to head downward
- But it bet that CDO tranches of the same bond portfolio with different ratings would diverge (capital structure arbitrage – long AAA and short BBB)
- The crisis drove down the value of high rated senior tranches
- Their investment banking creditors had liquidity problems of their own and could not accept further counterparty risk from Peloton, demanding additional collateral that Peloton was unable to meet; it had to liquidate the fund as a result
- The fund was also highly leveraged

Discuss the collapse of Carlyle Capital Corporation, the due diligence issues related to it, and lessons learned from the case

- Created by the Carlyle Group in 2007 as a way for the public to get exposure to some of its funds
- The fund died just 8 months after being listed on Euronext Amsterdam
- Strategy: borrowed significantly (31 to 1) at low short-term rates and invested in AAA-rated mortgage bonds issued by Fannie and Freddie whose values plummeted in February and March 2008
- CCC was hit with margin calls and seized its collateral and assets

Discuss the surprising decline of Marin Capital, the due diligence issues related to it, and lessons learned from the case

- Strategies that have been successful for many years have a special risk related to declining trading opportunities and increasing leverage
- Marin Capital was a convertible bond arbitrage fund (long debt, short equity of the same company) that was hit when in 2005 GM debt was downgraded two levels to BB and Ford was downgraded one level to BB+ from previous investment grade ratings
- Adding more pain, Kirk Krekorian announced that he would acquire a large stake in GM causing the stock price to spike
- Its losses in 2005 were minor in relation to huge gains in prior years but the fund closed voluntarily

Discuss the link between declining investment opportunities and use of leverage

- Strategies that have been successful for many years have a special risk related to declining trading opportunities and increasing leverage

Apply the concepts of return on equity, return on assets, and leverage to evaluate levered investment situations

- ROE = (ROA*L) – [r * (L-1)]
  - L = Leverage; if leverage is 2 to 1, then L = 200%
  - r = interest expense on its leverage

Identify and describe behavioral biases and their potential effects on risk taking

- Confirmation bias and anchoring are examples of behavioral biases

26.2 Demonstrate knowledge of major fund failures caused by fraud.

For example:

Discuss the case of Bayou Management (est.1996), the due diligence issues related to it, and lessons learned from it

- Bayou Capital set up a separate broker (Bayou Securities) to process trades and earn commissions – bad practice to earn commissions on trades of funds that they manage
- Fund performance was bolstered by rebates of commissions
- As losses continued, CEO Sam Israel and CFO Dan Marino falsified client statements even fabricating audits through a fictitious accounting firm Richmond-Fairfield Associates
- It then liquidated the Bayou Fund and created four successor funds to attract more capital
- It eventually stopped trading and transferred funds to their personal accounts
- Claiming a 1997 start date instead of 1996 enabled it to hide early losses
- A background check would have revealed that Israel overstated his previous employment positions

Discuss the case of Bernie Madoff, the due diligence issues related to it, and lessons learned from it

- Giant $50B Ponzi scheme which used affinity fraud

- Markopolous blew the whistle on the scheme, by initially studying the firm's supposed option collar strategy (buys the underlying asset, writes a call option at the higher strike, buys a put option at the lower strike) which limits upside and downside
- The high returns and minimal volatility were not consistent with similar strategies in the market
- The fund AUM would generate trading volume way too large to the trading activity in the options market
- Madoff also brokered, cleared, administered and audited his own fund

Discuss the case of Lancer Group, the due diligence issues related to it, and lessons learned from it

- Hedge fund trading in mostly very small-cap equities using public and private shares
- Lancer did not offer transparency to investors and refused to identify portfolio holdings
- Through partnership agreements, Lancer was able to value illiquid holdings – violation of cardinal rule in operational risk management
- Employed window dressing, manipulating the market price of registered shares; small trades in he registered, tradable shares were used to value unregistered shares
- 13D were not filed for over 5% stakes in companies

26.3 Demonstrate knowledge of lessons drawn from analysis of fund failures.

For example:

Discuss themes and lessons that emerge from the analysis of various types of fund failures

- Leverage is a double-edged sword
- Dangers of convergence trading when prices move against you
- Banks and prime brokers tend to magnify liquidity problems when the client most needs liquidity assistance

Chapter 27: Risk Analysis

Keywords

Actual investment strategy: The investment strategy being implemented by the fund.

Business risk: The added risk caused by unexpected performance of the business team.

Computer algorithm: Set of procedures within the software that determines the decisions or other output that are generated.

Custody: The safekeeping of the cash and securities of a fund.

Dynamic positions: Positions that change through time by the execution of market transactions. Dynamic trading strategies can exhibit payoffs that are option-like.

Fund culture: A generally shared set of priorities and values within the fund's organization.

Gaming: Strategic behavior designed to generate gains at the expense of others within the rules of a particular system.

Investment management governance process: Set of procedures through which investment decisions are made.

Investment mandate: A statement of the allowable strategy, goals and risks of an investment program.

Investment process risk: Risk caused by imperfect application of the stated investment strategy.

Investment strategy: The sets of objectives, principles, techniques, and procedures used to construct and modify the fund's portfolio.

Operational errors: Mistakes made in the process of executing the fund's investment strategy.

Operational fraud: Any intentional, self-serving, deceptive behavior by an employee of the fund manager that is generally harmful to the investor.

Operational risk: Risk linked to the imperfect implementation of a stated investment strategy.

Permitted investment strategies: The range of investment strategies that the fund's managers have communicated and are mandated as allowable for the fund to implement.

Position limit: A specific restriction on the size of the holdings of a particular security or combination of securities.

Risk limits: Maximum levels of measured risk that are allowed in the portfolio.

Rogue trader: Authorized employee making unauthorized trades (or just trades well outside the investment mandate) on behalf of their employer.

Slack variable: A variable that is added to an inequality constraint to transform it to an equality. It's also the variable in an optimization problem that takes on whatever value is necessary to allow an optimum to be feasible.

Stated investment strategy: The investment strategy that a diligent investor would expect the fund to pursue, based on a reasonable analysis of available information.

Style drift: The divergence of a fund from its stated investment style or objective.

Synergistic risk effect: The potential for the combination of two or more risks to have a greater total risk than the sum of the individual risks.

Learning Objectives

27.1 Demonstrate knowledge of investment strategy risks.

For example:

Identify and describe style drift risk

- The risk of a fund's strategy changing through time

27.2 Demonstrate knowledge of market risk.

For example:

Contrast the general and narrower definitions of market risk

- General: Market risk describes any risk attributable to changes in market prices and rates (includes systematic and idiosyncratic risk). This course focuses on this definition of market risk.
- Narrower: Market risk is used synonymously with systematic risk to refer to the portion of an asset's total risk that is attributable to changes in the value of the market portfolio or to a return factor that drives general market returns

Discuss potential interactions of market risk with other investment risks

- Even if market risk can be detected, investors may not be able to request and effect a return of their investment before the market has incurred substantial losses due to other risks (e.g., liquidity, etc.)

Describe the market risk of a stated investment strategy

- Any fund's stated investment strategy has market/systematic risk represented by one or more beta exposures and idiosyncratic risk represented by the volatility of the nonsystematic sources of risk

Compare the market risks of stated and actual investment strategies

- Stated investment strategies: How the fund is designed to behave (ex ante)
- Actual investment strategies: How the fund behaves in practice (ex post)

27.3 Demonstrate knowledge of operational risk.

For example:

Discuss two interpretations of operational risk

- Operational risk focuses on idiosyncratic risk of the fund
- Broad definition: Any deviation of the actual return of the fund from the return of the stated strategy.
- Specific definition: Focuses on the view of the fund's operations as excluding the investment process and the business side of the fund. Focuses on middle-office and back office operations.

Identify and describe operational errors

- Mistakes made in executing the fund's investment strategy
- Can be exacerbated by market risk

Identify and describe types of agency conflicts

- Rogue trader: Most often caused by strong incentives to generate performance, combined with losses that jeopardize a trader's career if not recouped
- Gaming: Efforts intended to generate gains to the agents capitalizing on flaws in the compensation structure

Identify and describe operational fraud

- Any deceptive behavior by fund employees that is harmful to the investor
- Can be reduced by a separation of duties (trading, risk management, accounting)

27.4 Demonstrate knowledge of investment process risk.

For example:

Discuss investment process risk and its detection

- Risk of imperfect application of the stated investment strategy by the investment team
- The difference between the proper implementation of the strategy and actual implementation
- Can be detected using quantitative analysis – analyzing historical returns versus market indices and similar funds to determine the extent to which the returns are consistent

Describe how style drift relates to investment process risk

- Style drift is a major component of investment process risk as it may allow a fund manager to stray into markets where he has less expertise

Discuss the process risk of implementing an investment strategy

- The process of implementing an investment strategy (sourcing ideas, setting leverage, executing trades, etc.) from concept to actual portfolio involves risk

27.5 Demonstrate knowledge of methods for controlling the operational risk of an investment.

For example:

Explain how incentives can increase operational risk

- Incentives that motivate a fund manager to report high and consistent performance can cause negative consequences
- There is an incentive for fund managers to reduce risk after substantial profits have accrued to lock in an acceptable level of performance and continued asset management

- The call option-like nature of performance-based fees incentivizes fund managers to take high risks; the incentive is greatest when the fund is near or below its high water mark

Discuss how internal control procedures can detect and reduce operational risk

- Risk limits and position limits can detect and reduce operational risk

Explain the importance of valuation procedures and independence in the valuation process

- Traders and fund managers should not value their own fund holdings for reporting purposes but this should be done through an independent process
- Managers may have an incentive to obscure losses to avoid reporting inferior returns and provide time to recoup losses; they may also have an incentive to smooth returns

Discuss concerns related to the custody of a fund's assets

- Are controls in place to prevent the movement of funds into fund manager personal accounts?
- Managed or separate accounts can provide the safest and most transparent arrangement for investors; the investor retains custody making it almost impossible for the fund manager to withdraw the funds

Identify and describe the concept of fund culture and how it affects operational risk

- A fund's culture may provide insight into the integrity of the fund manager

27.6 Demonstrate knowledge of the total risk of a fund.

For example:

Explain the difference between investment, operational, and business risk

- Investment risk: Involves all aspects of determining and implementing investment decisions.
- Operational risk: Middle and back office
- Business risk: Normal activities of running the organization (HR, technology, facilities)

Recognize and explain how leverage, strategy risk, and operational risk affect the total fund risk and return

- The total return of a fund can be represented as a product of three components
- $(1+R_{fund}) = (1+R_{strat}) * Leverage*(1+R_{or})$
- R_{fund} = actual total return of a fund
- R_{strat} = return on the unleveraged, stated investment strategy of the fund
- R_{or} = the percentage effect of all types of operational risk

Identify and describe synergistic risk effects

- Due to synergistic risk effects, the combination of two or more risks may have a greater total risk than the sum of the individual risks

- Formula below calculates standard deviation of the fund's actual return
- The idea here is that the total fund risk depends on the operational risks of the fund
- $\sigma\text{fund} = \text{Leverage} * \sqrt{\sigma_{strat}^2 + \sigma_{or}^2 + 2\rho_{strat,or} * \sigma_{strat} * \sigma_{or}}$
- $\rho_{strat,or}$ = correlation coefficient between R_{strat} and R_{or}; reflects the degree to which a fund's strategy drift, leverage decision or operational errors are related to the magnitude and direction of market returns
- σ_{strat} = standard deviation of the returns of the unleveraged stated investment strategy
- σ_{or} = standard deviation of the operational risk factor

Discuss the optimal levels of operational risk

- Balance the goal of optimal risk management with the cost

27.7 Demonstrate knowledge of risk analysis for portfolios of options.

For example:

Show how put-call parity can be used to form a riskless hedge

- Rearranges put-call parity relationship to show that a call, a put and a position in the underlying can form a riskless hedge
- +Stock + Put – Call = Riskless Bond

Discuss sensitivities of individual option positions and portfolios

	+Stock	+Put	+Call	+Stock + Put – Call
Delta	1	Call option delta - 1	Call option delta (σ)	0
Gamma	0	Gamma of a call option (γ)	Gamma of a call option (γ)	0
Vega	0	Vega of a call option (υ)	Vega of a call option (υ)	0

Explain how sensitivities of portfolios containing options can be managed

- If the underlying is gamma and vega neutral, and if (+Stock + Put – Call) is gamma and vega neutral, then the difference (Put – Call) must also be gamma and vega neutral
- Being long a call and short a put OR being long a put and short a call is hedged with respect to gamma risk and vega risk but leaves delta risk at either +1 or -1

Discuss how options can be used as volatility bets

- From the trader's perspective, the only difference between a call and a put is the delta and the trader can just expand or contract the hedging position in the underlying asset to maintain a zero net delta
- The trader can short vega and gamma with short positions in either calls or puts
- The position in the underlying asset is viewed as the slack variable used to control delta
- Some traders use options to place directional bets on the underlying assets

- Some sophisticated traders take the other side of these bets when they perceive that volatility is overpriced
- These traders maintain delta neutrality and therefore view the positions in mispriced options as pure bets on volatility that offer alpha
- Many strategies involve dynamic positions

Chapter 28: Due Diligence of Fund Managers

Keywords

Annual volatility: Only 16 times larger than daily volatility ($\sqrt{256}$) based on 256 trading days per year.

Attorneys: Typically responsible for keeping current all regulatory registrations of the fund manager and for preparing the fund manager's offering document.

Auditors: Auditor opinions other than "unqualified" must be understood.

Bias blind spot: The cognitive bias of failing to compensate for one's own cognitive biases.

Chief Risk Officer: Oversees the fund manager's program for identifying, measuring, monitoring and managing risk.

Daily volatility: With perfect autocorrelation, annual volatility is about 256 times higher than daily volatility.

Due diligence: The process of performing a review of an investment.

Expectation bias: The tendency for experimenters to believe, certify, and publish data that agree with their expectations for the outcome of an experiment, and to disbelieve, discard, or downgrade the corresponding weightings for data that appear to conflict with those expectations.

Gaming: Investment activity driven by a desire to generate favorable statistical measures of performance rather than driven by a desire to benefit investors.

Gate: A restriction placed on a hedge fund limiting the amount of withdrawals from the fund during a redemption period. The purpose of the provision is to prevent a run on the fund, which could cripple its operations, as a large number of withdrawals from the fund would force the manager to sell off a large number of positions.

Hard lock up period: In a hard lock-up, investors have no right to redeem before their time is up. In a soft lock-up, they can get out early but have to pay a redemption fee of, say, 3-5%.

Herd behavior: Describes how individuals in a group can act together without planned direction.

Information filtering: One of the information-based explanations for superior investment performance that describes a manager's ability to filter and analyze information to deliver superior returns.

Information gathering: One of the information-based explanations for superior investment performance when a manager has better access to information that allows a competitive edge.

Investment objective: The goals, nature and strategies of a fund's investment program.

Investment process: Methods the fund uses to formulate, execute and monitor investment decisions.

Key personnel clause: Provision that allows investors to withdraw their assets from a fund, immediately and without penalty, when the identified key personnel are no longer making investment decisions for the fund.

League table: Listing of organizations, generated by a research or media firm, which ranks organizations by size, volume or other indicators of activity.

Limited liability shield: Legal construct that prevents creditors from pursuing restitution from investors beyond the capital that they invested.

Lockup period: Window of time in which investors of a hedge fund or other closely-held investment vehicle are not allowed to redeem or sell shares.

Mark to model: The practice of pricing a position or portfolio at prices determined by financial models, in contrast to allowing the market to determine the price.

Master trust: A trust that invests the assets of both the onshore and offshore funds in an identical manner so that both funds share the benefit of the fund manager's insights.

N-sigma event: An event that is N standard deviations from the mean.

Omega-score: Attempts to indicate operational risk and is computed as a function of a fund's age, size, past performance, volatility and fee structure.

Prime broker: Clears and finances trades for investment manager clients, provides research, arranges financing, and produces portfolio accounting.

Process risk: The potential loss from failure to properly execute the stated investment strategy.

Shorting volatility: Strategy where a fund manager sells calls or put options without an offsetting position.

Side pocket arrangement: A type of account used in hedge funds to separate illiquid assets from other more liquid investments. Once an investment enters a side pocket account, only the present participants in the hedge fund will be entitled to a share of it. Future investors will not receive a share of the proceeds in the event the asset's returns get realized.

Soft lockup period: In a hard lock-up, investors have no right to redeem before their time is up. In a soft lock-up, they can get out early but have to pay a redemption fee of, say, 3-5%.

Trade allocation: The priorities with which an attractive investment opportunity is distributed among the manager's various funds and accounts.

Learning Objectives

28.1 Demonstrate knowledge of the three questions critical to understanding the nature of a manager's investment program.

For example:

Define and describe due diligence processes related to investigation of investment objectives of hedge funds

- In what markets and assets does the fund invest?
- What is the fund's general investment strategy?
- What is the fund's benchmark?

Define and describe due diligence processes related to investigation of investment processes of hedge funds

- Algorithmic or discretionary?
- Process risk
- Key personnel clause

Define and describe due diligence processes related to investigation of how hedge fund managers add value

- What enables a manager to identify alpha?
- Why will alpha persist?
- Two primary information-based explanations for superior investment performance: information gathering and information filtering; to have and maintain a competitive investment edge based on information, a fund manager must demonstrate one or both of these advantages

Describe and contrast information gathering and information filtering

- Information gathering: Better access to information
- Information filtering: Better skill in analyzing information

28.2 Demonstrate knowledge of the due diligence of hedge fund structures.

For example:

Describe the main issues related to the review of a fund's organization

- Fund managers may have different investors based in different parts of the world
- If the fund is based outside of the investor's home country, the investor may have to pay taxes to two countries

Discuss the master trust account structure and recognize its uses by hedge funds

- An onshore fund can be set up for US residents and an offshore fund for non-US investors which is set up in a domicile that does not cause the non-US investors to be subject to double taxation
- The master trust account allows investors in both the onshore and offshore funds to benefit from the separation of funds because tax consequences flow appropriately to both investor

Explain the importance of reviewing fund managers' organizational structures

- The investor should review where the fund is located (HQ, nearest office) since time differences and travel costs may make due diligence more costly

Discuss separation of duties and how organizational charts can be used to evaluate it

- Investment, operations, and management functions should not be done by the same person
- The CFO should have a strong background in investments

Recognize the importance of reviewing and documenting regulatory registrations

- The investor should determine the date of the original registration and whether there are any civil, criminal or administrative actions outstanding

Describe evaluation and documentation of outside service providers including the auditor, attorneys, and the prime broker

- The investor should assess the competence and reputation of outside service providers
- Look at league tables

28.3 Demonstrate knowledge of the strategic review of a fund manager in the due diligence process.

For example:

Explain the importance of understanding the markets and securities in which the manager invests

- Some strategies are not so clear
- Determine the extent of the use of derivatives and short selling
- Shorting volatility (selling puts or calls)

Discuss the issues related to benchmarking of fund returns

- Manager skill cannot be adequately captured by a passive securities index
- Most fund managers have risk exposures that can't be explained well by the returns of a passive index (e.g., long-only index not an appropriate benchmark for long-short manager)
- Many fund managers use derivatives with nonlinear payout functions not reflected in benchmarks

Describe key considerations in the analysis of managers' competitive advantages and sources of investment ideas

- What makes the fund manager's process more attractive than that of other managers?

Describe key considerations in the review of managers' current portfolio positions

- Analyze the fund's long and short positions to determine the extent to which the fund is exposed to systematic and idiosyncratic risks
- The sources of risk exposure should correspond to the stated investment strategy

Describe key considerations in the review of the source of investment ideas

- The investor should also determine in which market conditions the fund manager's ideas work best

Discuss investment strategy capacity in the context of evaluating the structural risk

- Fund manager might dilute their skill by allowing more capital into the fund than is optimal

28.4 Demonstrate knowledge of the administrative review of funds.

For example:

Discuss the importance of due diligence on the ethical and legal history of fund employees

- Important to review not just civil or criminal actions but also professional conduct complains even if outside the financial industry
- This all provides insight into the fund manager's character

Discuss the reasons for review of the employee turnover

- A stable workforce may be one way to sustain a competitive advantage
- Turnover is distracting – it takes time, money to replace talent
- High turnover may indicate volatile leadership

Discuss ideal organization of investor relations

- Performance reporting, subscriptions and redemptions, increased investment and related meetings should be handled by the IR team and not the fund manager
- Allows the fund manager to focus on investing activities

Describe the importance of business continuity management

- Required for funds registered with the US or UK authorities
- Loss of trading and computing functionality can impact performance
- An inability to manage portfolios exposes a fund to increased risk especially during a turbulent market

28.5 Demonstrate knowledge of the procedure for conducting a performance review of a fund manager in the due diligence process.

For example:

Describe the behavioral biases that can interfere with performance analysis

- Confirmation bias, herd behavior, bias blind spot

Identify and discuss three important questions to ask regarding all assets controlled by the fund manager

- How long has the fund manager been actively managing each current and previous fund?
- Have the manager's performance results been consistent over time and across funds?
- How do the investment strategies of the funds compare and contrast?

Discuss the analysis of drawdowns

- Past drawdowns provide indications of past risk that should be carefully considered in the due diligence process
- It should also indicate the fund's response to periods of market stress, as well as the fund's relative sensitivities to market risk and idiosyncratic risk
- Large drawdowns in a market neutral fund may indicate a lack of manager skill

Identify and discuss the five issues related to the use of past data to predict future performance

- Accuracy: Are the measures accurate? Beware of expectation bias.
- Representativeness: Are the measures representative of the fund's total experience?
- Stationarity: Are past results likely to predict future results?
- Gaming: Are the performance numbers gamed (driven by a desire to generate favorable statistical measures)?
- Appropriateness: Are the performance measures appropriate given the strategy?

Discuss issues related to subscriptions, redemptions, and volatility of assets under management

- If a fund is fully invested during large redemptions, performance typically suffers. Redemption also triggers transaction costs that are usually borne by all investors
- Rising subscriptions can also negatively impact performance:
  - Since it may take more time to get invested in the less liquid ideas, cash may be a drag on performance
  - Subscriptions cause transaction costs that are typically borne by all investors
  - Manager's best ideas may reach capacity

Describe considerations in the review of the asset manager's process for pricing securities in a portfolio

- There are conflicts of interest in establishing securities prices
- External pricing services are often used to reduce the opportunity to manipulate securities prices
- Even publicly traded securities prices can be manipulated
- Mark-to-model used for nonpublic securities

28.6 Demonstrate knowledge of the procedure for conducting a portfolio risk review of a fund manager in the due diligence process.

For example:

Identify and discuss three important risk management questions

- What are the types and levels of risk involved in the fund manager's strategy?
- What risks are measured, monitored and managed?
- How are risks measured, monitored and managed?

Describe the role of leverage in determining the total risk of a fund

- Leverage can magnify risk and return
- A fund with a leverage factor or ratio of L (assets/equity) has short-run returns that have L times the volatility of its assets
- N-sigma event (a two sigma event is two standard deviations from the mean)

Discuss the role of the Chief Risk Officer (CRO)

- Oversees the fund manager's program for identifying, measuring, monitoring and managing risk
- The CIO and CRO should not be the same person

28.7 Demonstrate knowledge of the procedure for conducting a legal review of a fund manager in the due diligence process.

For example:

Discuss considerations in the review of the fund structure

- Most are structured as limited partnerships (limited liability shield)
- Separate accounts typically do not offer limited liability

Discuss considerations in the review of the fund fees

- Look for high water marks and clawbacks as well as resets or look-back options
- Clawbacks and hurdle rates are rare in the hedge fund world but common in private equity

Discuss considerations in the review of the lockup and redemption provisions, including gates and hard and soft lockup periods

- Lockup periods can provide two benefits: 1. Give the fund manager time to implement the investment strategy and 2. Limit withdrawals by one LP that will disadvantage the other LPs through transaction costs
- Funds may require a hard or soft lockup period
- Gating typically occurs during times of market turbulence and constrained liquidity

Discuss considerations in the review of the subscription amount

- Most funds have a minimum subscription amount
- Funds may have safe harbor provisions limiting the number of investors
- Higher capital commitments help ensure that only sophisticated investors with a large net worth subscribe to the fund

- Some funds also have a maximum subscription amount so that no single investor becomes too large

Discuss the role of the advisory committee

- Source of objective input for the fund manager (on issues such as valuation, fund capacity)
- Comprised of representatives and investors in the fund
- More popular with private equity than with hedge funds

28.8 Demonstrate knowledge of the procedure for conducting reference checks on service providers and other fund investors.

For example:

Discuss the process of conducting reference checks on service providers

- Prime broker: Inquire regarding financing arrangements, margin call policy (size and frequency)
- Auditors: Whether an unqualified opinion was issued

Identify key questions to ask when conducting reference checks on other investors

- Done to check investor satisfaction and the truth in the fund manager's statements
- Have the financial reports been timely and easy to understand?
- Would you invest more money with the manager?

28.9 Demonstrate knowledge of the procedure for measuring operational risk.

For example:

Discuss the role of the omega-score in measuring operational risk

- Follows general approach of corporate bankruptcy models and credit scoring models

Discuss the cost of fund manager due diligence

- It's expensive in terms of money and time spent
- Costs also driven by the extent of the use of third-party service providers
- Due diligence costs can run $50,000 to $100,000 per fund

Chapter 29: Regression, Multivariate, and Nonlinear Methods

Keywords

Auto correlation: A mathematical representation of the degree of similarity between a given time series and a lagged version of itself over successive time intervals.

Conditional correlation: Correlation between two variables under specified circumstances.

Dependent variable: The predicted variable in a regression model.

Goodness of fit: The extent to which the model appears to explain the variation in the dependent variable. R^2 is often used to assess goodness of fit.

Hedge fund replication: Process of identifying an investment strategy that mimics the returns of a particular hedge fund.

Heteroskedasticity: Residual variance related to level of independent variables. In the case of heteroskedasticity, the variance of residuals is not the same across all observations and there are subsamples more spread out than rest of the sample.

Multicollinearity: When independent variables in a regression model are correlated with each other.

Multiple regression model: The multiple regression model specifies a dependent variable as a linear function of two or more independent variables. The intercept term is the value of the dependent variable when the independent variables are equal to zero. Each slope coefficient is the estimated change in the dependent variable for a one-unit change in that independent variable, holding the other independent variables constant.

Negative conditional correlation: When correlation falls in rising markets and rises in falling markets.

Non-stationary: When return volatilities and/or correlations vary through time. A time series is covariance stationary if its mean, variance, and covariances with lagged and leading values do not change over time.

Outliers: Values that are unusually large or small. May influence the results of regression and the estimate of the correlation coefficient. Excluding outliers may reduce correlation number.

Positive conditional correlation: When correlations are lower during down markets and larger during rising markets.

Principal components analysis: Statistical technique that groups the observations in a large data set into smaller sets of similar types. It identifies subgroups of observations that tend to behave similarly.

Regression: Linear regression provides an estimate of the linear relationship between an independent variable (the explanatory variable) and a dependent variable (the predicted variable).

R-square: Also called the coefficient of determination, R^2, is the proportion of the total variation of the dependent variable explained by the regression. An R^2 of 60.53% means that 60.53% of the variation in Y (dependent variable) is explained by the variation in X (independent variable).

Simple linear regression: In simple linear regression, there is only one independent variable.

Slope coefficient: The estimated slope coefficient is interpreted as the change in the dependent variable for a 1-unit change in the independent variable.

Stepwise regression: Regression models in which the choice of predictive variables is carried out by an automatic procedure. It is an iterative technique where variables are added or deleted based on their statistical significance.

Style analysis: Process of understanding an investment strategy, especially using a statistical approach.

Learning Objectives

29.1 Demonstrate knowledge of single-factor regression models.

For example:

Explain the use of ordinary least squares to estimate regression parameters

- Ordinary least squares regression selects the intercept and slope that minimizes the sum of the squared values of the residuals
- This method has been shown to generate unbiased estimates of if the error terms in the model are:
  - Normally distributed
  - Uncorrelated
  - Homoscedastic

Describe the problem outliers pose to regression analysis

- Fat tails (leptokurtic distributions) are the same as frequent outliers
- Large outliers cause the slope and intercept estimates to be driven too much by the outliers rather than by more representative data

Describe the problem that autocorrelation poses to regression analysis

- Violations of the assumption that the error terms are uncorrelated through time occur most often when the returns are autocorrelated
- Many alternative investment returns are prone to autocorrelation due to smoothed pricing or illiquidity
- Can test for autocorrelation using the Durbin-Watson test

Describe the problem that heteroskedasticity poses to regression analysis

- Heteroskedasticity is when the variance of the error term varies
- Can be detected visually by examining scatter plots
- The most popular correction is weighted least squares

Recognize and apply the CAPM-based regression

- The ex post version of CAPM describes realized excess returns as a function of the market beta, the market portfolio's realized excess return, and an error term that reflects idiosyncratic risk
- The CAPM-based regression equation for asset i based on a time series of total return data is:
  - $R_{it} - R_f = a_i + b_{i,m}[R_{mt} - R_f] + e_{it}$
  - R_{it} = return of the asset i in time t
  - a_i = estimated intercept
  - $b_{i,m}$ = estimated slope coefficient
  - R_{mt} = market return
  - R_f = risk-free rate

Interpret results of a regression analysis using the CAPM as an example

- The CAPM-based regression equation attempts to explain values of the dependent variable ($R_{it} - R_f$) through movements in the independent variable ($R_{mt} - R_f$).
- $b_{i,m}$ = estimated slope coefficient and an estimate of market beta

29.2 Demonstrate knowledge of multiple-factor regression models.

For example:

Recognize and apply the ex post version of the Fama-French model

- CAPM assumes that market exposure is the only risk that is priced
- When analyzing alternative investments, a variety of risk factors can explain returns; must be careful when interpreting an estimated intercept as alpha because any omitted risk factors may be falsely attributed to alpha
- $R_{it} - R_f = a_i + b_{mi}(R_{mt} - R_f) + b_{1i}(R_{st} - R_{bt}) + b_{2i}(R_{ht} - R_{it}) + e_{it}$
- $R_{mt} - R_f$ = excess return on market
- $R_{st} - R_{bt}$ = size factor
- $R_{ht} - R_{it}$ = value factor
- The result of adding more *true* factors to the model is that R^2 goes up and the alpha estimate declines

Describe the problem that multicollinearity poses to multiple-factor regression analysis

- When independent variables are correlated to each other
- It can be tough to estimate the slope coefficients as the standard errors are inflated by the simultaneous presence of the correlated variables
- With multicollinearity, it can be difficult to find independent variables with coefficients that have significant t-statistics even when R^2 is high

Discuss the selection process of independent variables for multiple-factor regression analysis and the potential shortcomings to the stepwise regression technique

- A stepwise regression technique is more appropriate rather than just including all potential variables in the regression
- However, the stepwise regression technique could result in data dredging as searching across large data sets with numerous potential independent variables can locate statistically significant relationships over the time period of the regression but those results may not explain the dependent variable using data from outside the sample
- Overfitted models (too many variables) explain the past well but do not predict future relationships well

29.3 Demonstrate knowledge of nonlinear return models.

For example:

Recognize and apply dynamic risk exposure models

- These models model the dynamic nature of an alternative fund's return exposure to the market with very specific schemes
- The profits/losses of a perfect market timer that profits from a market move in either direction would be the same as having a free long positions in option straddles (long call, long put, same strike price)
- The diagram of profit or loss against market returns would be a perfect V shape, with the bottom of the V on the origin (where the x and y axis meet)
- $R_{it} - R_f = a_i + \{[b_{i,u} + (D_1 * b_{i,diff})] * (R_{mt} - R_f)\} + e_{it}$
  - D (dummy variable): set to 1 when excess returns on market index is negative and set to 0 when it's non-negative
  - In up markets the coefficient of excess returns is $b_{i,u}$
  - In down markets the coefficient of excess returns is $b_{i,u} + b_{i,diff}$
  - $b_{i,diff}$ = the difference between the up market and down market betas

Identify and apply statistical models that estimate the market timing skill of fund managers

- $R_{it} - R_f = a_i + b_{i,m}(R_{mt} - R_f)^2 + e_{it}$
- Generates a U-shaped profit-loss diagram
- The squared value of the excess return on the market is used to explain the performance of the fund's excess return
- A positive beta indicates market timing skill

29.4 Demonstrate knowledge of methods for modeling changing correlation.

For example:

Recognize and describe conditional correlation

- The behavior being measured is based on or only applies to a limited set of circumstances (e.g., observed only in markets up 1% or more)
- Conditional correlation is constant across conditions when the relationship between two variables is completely linear

Apply the concept of conditional correlation

- Negative conditional correlation: When correlation falls in rising markets and rises in falling markets; undesirable for investors since they want less correlations during times of market turbulence
- Positive conditional correlation: The only indices to exhibit this were equity market neutral and managed futures

Describe the rolling window approach to modeling changing correlation

- Advanced analysis for analyzing the change in market exposures over time
- Uses a time width for the window (e.g., 36 months) and performs the regression analysis for each contiguous 36-month period in the data

- Using 10 years of data with a window of 36 months would produce 85 unique regression outputs
- The first regression would use the data from months 1-36, then 2-37 and finally 85-120
- The output of each regression would show the estimated relationship between the dependent and independent variables over time

29.5 Demonstrate knowledge of approaches to analyzing fund returns using multi-factor models.

For example:

Describe how asset classes can be used to analyze returns of a fund

- Style analysis
- Sharpe results indicated that 90% of each mutual fund's returns are based on the returns of a few underlying asset classes

Describe how strategy index returns can be used in style analysis

- The returns to the mutual funds can be attributed to the returns of indices corresponding to traditional financial security classes related to the most common holdings of the mutual fund

Describe how a fund's returns can be analyzed using returns of similar funds

- Grouping funds by styles and analyzing the returns of funds with the returns of other funds of similar style is commonly done with both traditional and alternative investments
- Principal components analysis
- Fung and Hsieh found that the returns of many hedge funds fell into one of five trading styles: 1. Systems/opportunistic 2. Global/macro 3. Value 4. Systems/trend following 5. Distressed

Describe how market-wide factors can be used to analyze returns of a fund

- Fama-French
- The factors in a Fama-French style of analysis are tradable since you can be long one factor (small-cap stocks) and short another (large-cap stocks)

Describe how specialized market factors can be used to analyze returns of a fund

- Related to hedge fund replication

Describe hedge fund replication and how it relates to modeling of fund returns

- Hedge fund replication in this sense can be used to identify specialized market factors and estimate fund exposures to those factors such that a portfolio of other securities can be constructed that generates beta similar to a selected fund

29.6 Demonstrate knowledge of hedge fund performance persistence.

For example:

Discuss approaches to estimating hedge fund performance persistence (is good performance repeatable?)

- Examine the correlation between past and future returns
- Develop objective measures of skill in another period
- Look at the persistence of volatility in hedge fund returns
- Measure the serial correlation among the returns to hedge funds

Chapter 30: Portfolio Optimization and Risk Parity

Keywords

Dominant: If a portfolio has a higher expected return than another portfolio with the same level of risk, a lower level of expected risk than another portfolio with equal expected return or a higher expected return and lower expected risk then the portfolio is dominant.

Efficient frontier: The efficient frontier is the positively sloped portion of the minimum-variance frontier. Portfolios on the efficient frontier have the highest expected return at each given level of risk.

Efficient portfolio: An efficient portfolio is one that lies on the efficient frontier. An efficient portfolio provides the lowest level of risk possible for a given level of expected return.

Equilibrium expected return: The expected return that causes the optimal weight of that security in investor portfolios to equal its market weight.

Feasible portfolio: Possible set of investments chosen from the available alternatives within the limits of the investor's capital resources, risk tolerance, and investment objectives. Each feasible portfolio has its own risk and reward profile, and is not necessarily an efficient portfolio.

Heuristic method: Simplified, practical but theoretically suboptimal strategy developed through time and experience to solve problems.

Hurdle rate: Expected rate of return that an asset must offer to be included in a portfolio.

Marginal risk contribution: The rate at which an additional unit of that asset would cause the portfolio's total risk to rise.

Risk budgeting: A broad spectrum of approaches to portfolio construction and maintenance that emphasize the determination of an aggregate level of risk and the selection of a portfolio based solely or primarily on risk.

Risk parity: Risk budgeting approach to investment portfolio management which focuses on allocation of risk, usually defined as volatility, rather than allocation of capital. The risk parity approach asserts that when asset allocations are adjusted (leveraged or deleveraged) to the same risk level, the risk parity portfolio can achieve a higher Sharpe ratio and can be more resistant to market downturns than the traditional portfolio.

Two-fund separation theorem: The theoretical result that all investors will hold a combination of the risk-free asset and the market portfolio.

Learning Objectives

30.1 Demonstrate knowledge of mean-variance portfolio optimization.

For example:

Discuss and apply the methods for determining a portfolio's expected return and standard deviation

- Expected return = $E[R_p] = \sum_{i=1}^{n} w_i E[R_i]$
- $\sigma_p^2 = \sum_{i=1}^{n} \sum_{j=1}^{n} w_i w_j cov_{i,j}$
- For a 3-asset portfolio:
  - $\sigma_p^2 = w_1^2 \sigma_1^2 + w_2^2 \sigma_2^2 + w_3^2 \sigma_3^2 + 2w_1w_2cov_{1,2} + 2w_2w_3cov_{2,3} + 2w_1w_3cov_{1,3}$

Describe the efficient frontier and its application to mean-variance optimization

- Set of portfolios with the maximum return for each level of risk (σ)
- It is optimal to choose portfolios on or above the efficient frontier

Recognize and apply the objectives and constraints of the mean-variance portfolio optimization process

- Objective: maximize return or minimize risk
- Constraints:
  - Maximize expected return
  - Subject to: variance = target risk
  - $\sum_{i=1}^{n} w_i = 1$
  - $w_i \geq 0$

Describe the two-fund separation theorem

- Unlike mean-variance approach, incorporates the ability to use leverage to invest in the risky portfolio

Describe a hurdle rate and apply it to evaluate the addition of an asset to a portfolio

- An asset should be added to a portfolio when the following is true:
  - $E(R_c) > R_f + [E(R_p) - R_f] * (\sigma_c/\sigma_p) * \rho_{c,p}$
  - $E(R_c)$ = expected return of the asset under consideration
  - $E(R_p)$ = expected return of the existing portfolio
  - $\rho_{c,p}$ = correlation between the asset to be added and the current portfolio; this is a main variable that determines whether or not to add the asset to the portfolio

Discuss the advantages and disadvantages of mean-variance optimization, the CAPM, and two-fund separation in the context of determining optimal portfolios

- When asset returns are not normally distributed, investor preferences can't always be maximized based on mean and variance
- Investors can't make decisions based entirely on single-period outcomes when asset prices have varying means, standard deviations, and correlations through time

- Some assets are illiquid, investor mandate may require them to reduce the risk of shortfall

30.2 Demonstrate knowledge of complications to mean-variance optimization.

For example:

Describe the concept of mean-variance optimizers as "error maximizers"

- This is referring to the tendency of mean-variance portfolio optimizers to generate solutions with extreme portfolio weights (typically to the assets with the highest mean return and lowest volatility)

Describe how mean-variance optimizers ignore higher moments and explain how this complication can be addressed

- It does not model skewness and kurtosis
- When dealing with alternative investments, portfolio optimizers tend to suggest portfolios with desirable combinations of mean and variance but with highly undesirable skew and kurtosis

Describe how mean, variance, and covariance estimation errors affect mean variance optimization

- Erroneous forecasts of mean, variance, and covariance can result in extreme portfolio weights

Discuss extensions of and modifications to mean-variance optimization models

- Black-Litterman
  - Addresses the tendency of the user's estimates of mean and variance to generate extreme portfolio weights in a mean-variance optimizer
  - If a security offers an equilibrium expected return, then the demand for it will equal the supply
  - Equilibrium expected return concept
  - Allows for an analyst to adjust the mean return so that the suggested weights aren't so extreme
- Employ shrinkage techniques – adjust estimates of covariance to reduce the range and dispersion of covariance estimates
- Common additional constraints:
  - Limits on estimated tracking error of the optimal portfolio from the benchmark
  - Limits on divergences of portfolio weights from benchmark weights
  - Constraints on the estimated skewness and kurtosis of the optimal portfolio
  - Limits or ranges on the prescribed portfolio weights

30.3 Demonstrate knowledge of risk budgeting in portfolio construction.

For example:

Describe the specification of risk in the risk budgeting approach

- Risk budgeting requires a specification of how risk is measured

- o Standard deviation of returns
  - o Standard deviation of tracking error against a benchmark
  - o VaR
  - o Beta
- Risk budgeting does not require the specification of expected returns, although expected returns are used when the asset allocator is using the standard deviation of the tracking errors between the portfolio's return and a benchmark's return
- A popular application of risk budgeting allocates a portfolio between passive and active investments

Explain why risk budgeting does not emphasize return optimization

- This is the difference between risk budgeting and mean-variance optimization (which selects assets based on the trade-off between risk and return)
- Risk budgeting offers a heuristic portfolio strategy in which a portfolio is allocated completely or predominantly on risk, with little or no consideration to expected return because the available assets are selected based on the perceived attractiveness of their returns

Describe the process of risk budgeting in a CAPM framework

- Can allocate among assets based on betas and solve for a portfolio beta

30.4 Demonstrate knowledge of the risk parity approach to portfolio construction and maintenance.

For example:

Describe the risk parity approach

- See Keywords

Identify and describe the three steps to solving for risk parity

- Choose a definition for total risk (usually standard deviation)
- Choose a method to measure the marginal risk contribution of each asset class to the total risk of the portfolio
- Determine portfolio weights for the assets

Recognize an asset's marginal contribution to the total portfolio risk

- Marginal contribution of asset class i = MC_i = weight of asset class i $* \frac{\Delta Total\ risk\ of\ portfolio}{\Delta weight\ of\ asset\ class\ i}$
- Total risk measured by standard deviation (σ)

Recognize how the total risk of a portfolio can be expressed as the sum of the marginal risk contributions of its components

- $MC_1 = w_1 * (\frac{w_1 \sigma_1^2 + w_2 cov_{1,2}}{\sigma_p})$

- $MC_2 = w_2 * (\frac{w_2\sigma_2^2 + w_1 cov_{1,2}}{\sigma_p})$

Recognize how an asset's marginal contribution to the total portfolio risk can be expressed in terms of the beta of each asset with respect to the total portfolio

- $MC_i = w_i * \beta_i * \sigma_p$

Discuss the generation of portfolio weights using the risk-parity approach

- The total risk of a portfolio may be expressed as a sum of the marginal contributions of the assets
- The portfolio weights that equalize all of the marginal contributions to risk can be found using trial and error or an optimization approach (Solver in MS Excel)
- Can result in an over-allocation to asset classes like fixed income

Discuss the economic rationales for the risk-parity approach

- Lack of market efficiency and the existence of market imperfections make a risk-parity approach worthwhile
- A risk-parity approach provides a practical and easily implemented approach to selecting a low-volatility portfolio without the dangers of using a portfolio optimization technique

Provide examples of other approaches to forming low-risk portfolios

- Use mean-variance optimization to identify the minimum variance portfolio by finding the weights that minimize the return volatility
- A volatility-weighted portfolio can be used by weighting each asset *inversely* to its volatility

Discuss the characteristics of alternative investments in risk parity portfolios

- Allocations to alternative investments using a risk-parity approach will be relatively high given their low volatility and low correlation

Chapter 31: Portfolio Management, Alpha, and Beta

Keywords

Active return: Active return is the difference between portfolio and benchmark returns.

Active risk: active risk is the standard deviation of active return over time. Active risk is determined by the manager's active factor tilt and active asset selection decisions.

Actively managed portfolio: Portfolio management strategy where the manager makes specific investments with the goal of outperforming an investment benchmark index.

Distinguishing alpha and beta: Process of identifying how much of an asset's return is generated by alpha versus beta.

Enhanced index products: Products designed to take slightly more risk than the index within tightly controlled parameters and offer a little extra return, usually on a large pool of capital.

Index products: Products that take little or no active risk and are not expected to generate active return.

Passively managed portfolio: Investors expect a return that closely replicates the investment weighting and returns of a benchmark index.

Portable alpha: Return of an investment portfolio with zero market risk (beta). Being independent of both the direction and the magnitude of the market's movements, it represents the manager's skill in selecting investments. Elimination of the market risk can be accomplished by means of short selling and derivatives such as futures, swaps, and options.

Separating alpha and beta: Refers to portfolio management attempts to independently manage a portfolio's alpha and its exposure toward a desired level of beta.

Strategic asset allocation decision: A portfolio strategy that involves periodically rebalancing the portfolio in order to maintain a long-term goal for asset allocation.

Tactical asset allocation: An active management portfolio strategy that rebalances the percentage of assets held in various categories in order to take advantage of market pricing anomalies or strong market sectors.

Traditional approach to portfolio allocation: A long-term target allocation decision, known as the strategic asset allocation decision.

Zero-sum game: Market, environment, or situation in which any gains to one party must be equally offset by losses to one or more parties.

Learning Objectives

31.1 Demonstrate knowledge of factors involved in the estimation of alpha and beta.

For example:

Discuss errors in estimating ex ante alpha

- Alpha and beta are generally unobservable and need to be estimated based on historical data
- The analyst's estimate of alpha may vary significantly based on which outcome occurs
- Ex ante alpha is likely to be estimated with great error

Discuss errors in estimating beta

- Outliers can skew the data
- The beta's sign can be driven by randomness, depending on the strategy

Discuss the challenges and techniques of estimating dynamic alpha and beta (changing through time)

- Strategies may generate more or less alpha depending on the market environment
- No reason to forecast that the past beta will be similar to future beta

31.2 Demonstrate knowledge of the concept of separating alpha and beta.

For example:

Describe the concept of separation of alpha and beta

- May be viewed as a portfolio strategy and a portfolio management capability

31.3 Demonstrate knowledge of portable alpha.

For example:

Demonstrate how to transfer risk with appropriately-sized positions in derivatives

- Notional value for Hedging = Value of position to be hedged * Beta

Apply the concept of notional value to determine futures positions designed to transfer risk

- Number of contracts necessary $= \dfrac{Future\ contract\ notional\ value}{Index\ value * multiplier}$

Discuss the application of portable alpha

- The laying off of small-cap risk and the layering on of S&P500 risk can be accomplished using derivatives:
    - Invest cash in the small-cap strategy for its positive alpha
    - Take a short position in a small-cap index using a derivative (e.g., futures)

- o Take a long position in a derivative on the S&P500 to bring the total position into conformity with the benchmark (S&P500)

Apply the concept of portable alpha to portfolio management

- Do practice problems

Discuss challenges with porting alpha

- The challenges of estimating and forecasting alpha and beta make implementation of portable alpha more difficult
- Thus, the risk will be imperfectly hedged
- One approach to reducing the impact of estimation risk is to port the alpha of a portfolio of active managers rather than the alpha of just a single manager

31.4 Demonstrate knowledge of asset allocation using the concepts of alpha and beta.

For example:

Describe the process of traditional asset allocation

- Strategic vs. tactical asset allocation

Explain strategic and tactical asset allocation

- See Keywords

Describe the new investment model

- Investments are allocated with flexibility and in the explicit context of alpha and beta management

Discuss active risk and active returns for traditional investment products

- Active risk: the risk that an actively managed portfolio contains, as the portfolio manager tries to beat the benchmark. The variation in performance can be attributed to systematic risk that differs from the benchmark and idiosyncratic risk.
- Active returns: The expected or consistently realized return from active management relative to a passively managed portfolio or the benchmark.

Evaluate the proposition that alpha is a zero-sum game

- In order for this to be true, the following would have to be true (and are not):
  - o Investors have the same investment horizon
  - o Investors have the same level of risk tolerance
  - o Investors are allowed the same access to all asset classes
  - o Investors pay the same tax rate (or there is no tax)
  - o Investors can be divided and traded without cost
- Net positive alpha can be generated across time, asset classes and risk tolerances

Made in the USA
Middletown, DE
22 February 2021